AMERICA EATS

FORMS OF EDIBLE FOLK ART

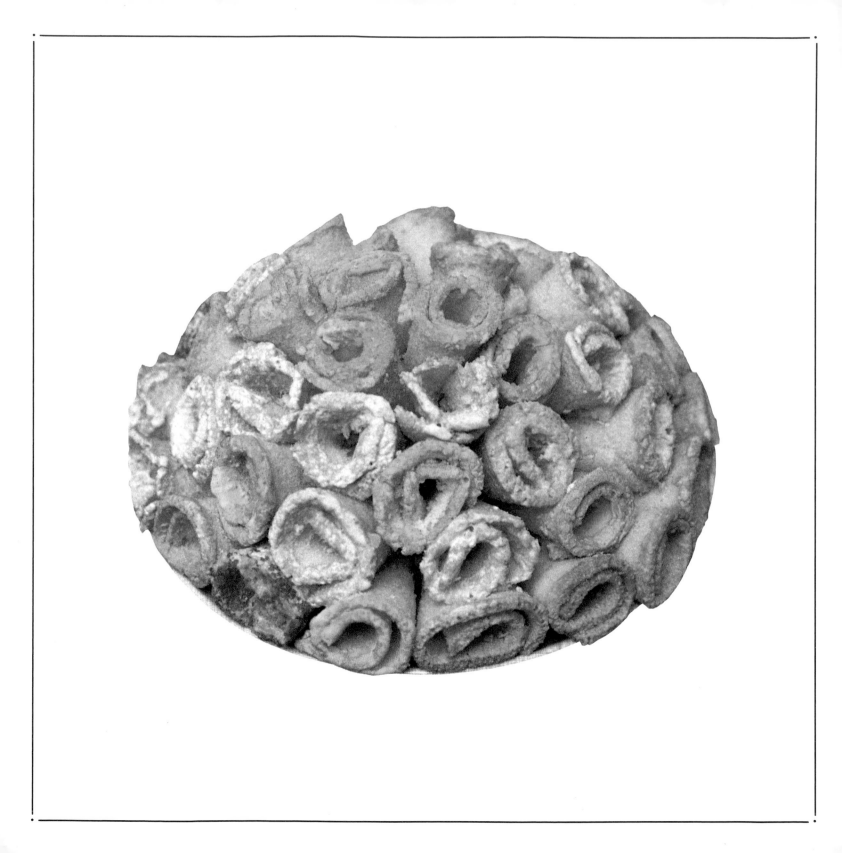

AMERICA EATS

FORMS OF EDIBLE FOLK ART

William Woys Weaver

MUSEUM OF AMERICAN FOLK ART

HARPER & ROW, PUBLISHERS, NEW YORK

GRAND RAPIDS, PHILADELPHIA, ST. LOUIS, SAN FRANCISCO, LONDON, SINGAPORE, SYDNEY, TOKYO, TORONTO

PERENNIAL LIBRARY

FRONTIS: **Morning Glory Cake by Norma Schrope.**

OPPOSITE PAGE: **Vegetable chopper, dated 1796. Courtesy of Independence National Historical Park, Philadelphia.**

Printed by South China Printing Company, Hong Kong.
FIRST EDITION

DESIGNED BY JOEL AVIROM

Library of Congress Cataloging-in-Publication Data
Weaver, William Woys, 1947–
    America eats: forms of edible folk art/William Woys Weaver.—1st ed.
        p.   cm.
    Bibliography: p.
    Includes index.
    ISBN 0-06-055177-1
    ISBN 0-06-096413-8 (pbk.)
    1. Cookery, American—Exhibitions.   2. Kitchen utensils—United States—Exhibitions.   I. Title.
TX715.W364   1989
641.5973—dc20   89-45116

89 90 91 92 93 SCP 10 9 8 7 6 5 4 3 2 1

89 90 91 92 93 SCP 10 9 8 7 6 5 4 3 2 1 (pbk.)

For Pat Guthman,
who long ago saw art in pots and pans

CONTENTS

List of Traditional Recipes
Tested for Today's Kitchen

BALTIMORE CRAB GUMBO (1893)

BOILED CIDER PIE (CA. 1865)

BOSTON BROWN BREAD (1873)

BRANDIED CHERRIES (1855)

CATFISH SOUP (1903)

CIDER JELLY (1891)

CORN DODGERS (1889)

CORN DROP DUMPLINGS (1897)

CRACKER HASH (1884)

DR. ESENWEIN'S TOMATO CATSUP (1912)

ELECTION CAKE (1874)

FRIED PEACHES (1885)

FUNERAL BISCUIT (1702)

GERMAN PICKLED TOMATOES (1870)

GREEN TOMATO PIE (1839)

GRILLED TURKEY (1891)

GUMBIS (1842)

HAM AND PARSNIPS (BEFORE 1822)

HIGDOM (1892)

HOMINY BREAD (1870)

HONEY TEA CAKE (BEFORE 1834)

HOPPIN JOHN (1907)

MAPLE CANDY (1894)

MARYLAND BISCUIT (1894)

MUSH MUFFINS (1915)

NEW ENGLAND PANCAKES (1787)

NEW YEAR'S CAKE (1834)

NEW YORK POTASH CAKE (1821)

PEPPER AND MELON MANGOES (1914)

PERSIMMON PUDDING (1915)

PICKLED EGGS (1868)

PRESERVED CITRON (1848)

QUAIL POT PIE (1917)

SALEM FANCY CAKE (1833)

SCOTT'S NEW YORK CHOWDER (1865)

SPIDER CORN CAKE (1887)

TRAINING CAKE (1874)

TRENCH STEW (1924)

VINEGAR PIE (1883)

WINTER SAUSAGE (1845)

WISCONSIN CAKES (1865)

WORCESTER LOAF (1854)

America Eats is about the culinary heart of the American people. It is about the relationship of folk cookery, the cookery of the common man, to folk art and the kinship these two ideas share when they come together in the American kitchen.

This process, this coming together, evolved over the past three centuries as Europeans, Africans, and American Indians shared ingredients, ideas, and techniques. This hybridizing rapidly gave birth to several distinctive regional cultures and regional cookeries, among them the "northern" or New England, the Middle Atlantic, and the tidewater or coastal South. From these original settlement areas, waves of American-born settlers carried ideas, food habits, and distinctive cookeries westward across the continent. They extended colonial cultures geographically but also planted seeds for innovation in the American heartland. Thus, this is also a book about evolution and continuity, about how folk cookery adapted to such things as changes of environment and shifts in kitchen technologies.

In spite of the fact that American folk cookery exists everywhere in the country and is three centuries old, its serious study is relatively recent. This book and its companion exhibit at the Museum of American Folk Art in New York are intended to bring together what we know about American folk cookery—the implements, the ideas, the recipes, and the techniques—and redefine this in terms of craftsmanship. The folk cook of the past, standing by her hearth or cast-iron stove, is treated as the mistress of a recognizable art. While rooted in oral tradition, hers is a form of training that shares many of the same principles as the fine arts. And yet, for all its simplicity, it is also complex because it is familial and deals directly with basic human experiences centered on the table.

This brings into play an enormous range of emotional stimuli and interactions. In fact, it is the emotional framework or setting that gives folk cookery much of its distinctive character. On the one hand, it embraces something I call "connectedness," the implicit overlapping of nature and kitchen, as in Thomas Hicks's painting of a woman paring freshly picked quinces by a rustic Long Island hearth. On the other hand, it is the boisterous "ethnicity" of a Polish-American wedding. As we shall see, the substance and emotional dimension of folk cookery are constantly changing and therefore are in constant need of

Pumpkin pie is the patriotic theme for the cover of a cookbook issued by the patent medicine firm of C. I. Hood in 1892. (Roughwood Collection)

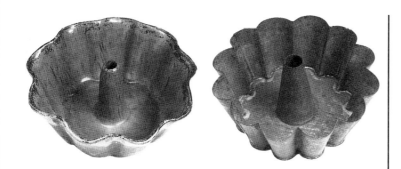

Sponge cake pans in redware *(left)* and tin *(right)*,
Pennsylvania, nineteenth century.

PAGE XII: *Kitchen Interior* by Thomas Hicks (1865).
Courtesy of IBM Corporation, Armonk, New York.

redefinition. At the heart of folk cookery
lies adaptation, the art of re-creating the
old in new and different combinations.

Even though this book is a companion
volume to an exhibit, it is intended to
stand by itself, to have a life of its own far
beyond that of the physical installation.
And even though many of the objects and
utensils illustrated on the following pages
are also part of the exhibit, this is not a
catalogue by any measure. It is a general
discussion of themes interspersed with examples. With that in mind, it is my underlying hope that my discussions will serve
as a useful reference for a wide range of
readers, from serious collectors of culinaria,
to my many friends out there who simply
love to cook.

For the collector, I have included a detailed list of objects illustrated in the book;
this information represents the fruit of several years of research. For the cook, I have
included recipes for many of the dishes discussed in the text, often to show a specific
relationship between an implement and the
food it was intended to contain or to make.
In this respect, the forty-two recipes represent forty-two ways for you to sample history in your own kitchen.

In addition, they provide forty-two ways
that you and I can share in the mutual
experience of cooking together, even
though we may be many miles apart. This
sharing of experience, this standing in
mind and spirit side by side over our pots
and pans, of establishing our American kinship without spoken words, will be one of
our first lessons in folk cookery. I say "our"
because folk cookery is part of all of us,
whether or not our ancestors came here
three centuries ago. The "classical" folk
cookery of early America was based on
connectedness, an affiliation with place, a
direct link with nature, and a strong bond
between people. These are qualities that go
beyond time and cultural boundaries.

William Woys Weaver
Guest Curator
Museum of American Folk Art

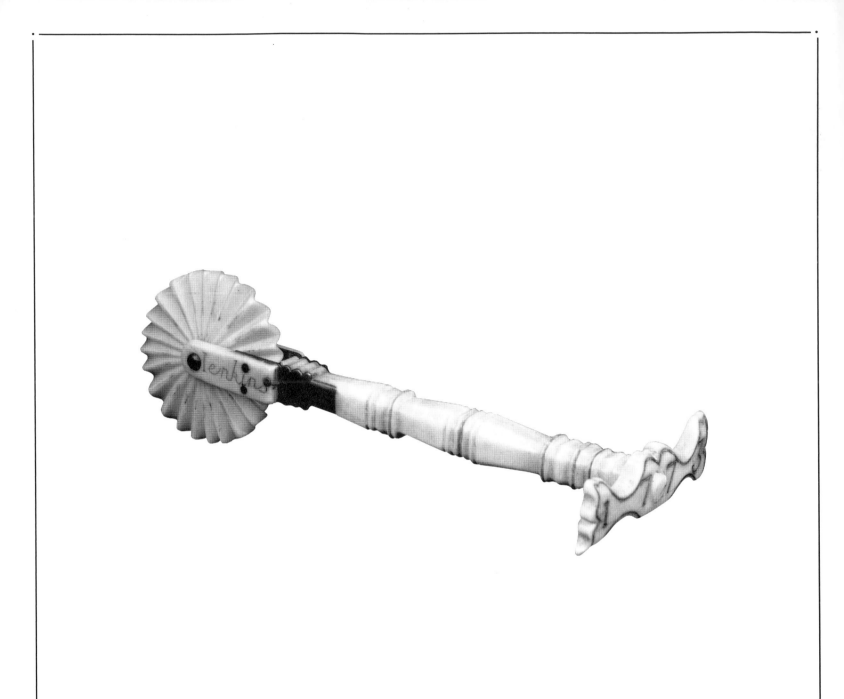

Nantucket pie crimper of walrus ivory. Dated 1773.
Courtesy of the Museum of Art, Rhode Island
School of Design.

Acknowledgments

There were a large number of museums and private collectors who provided me with bits and pieces for this book and who enthusiastically came to my aid when it finally came time to choose objects, make photographs, and, yes, to help out when I needed just a little more advice.

Jack Lindsey of the Philadelphia Museum of Art and Joan Whitlow of the Essex Institute, Salem, Massachusetts, stand out for the very special attention they gave to my quite unconventional requirements. I should also mention Frank White of Old Sturbridge Village, Sturbridge, Massachusetts, and Dennis Moyer of the Schwenkfelder Library in Pennsburg, Pennsylvania, for help far beyond the call of duty. The other museums that must be thanked include The Anglo-American Art Museum, Louisiana State University, Baton Rouge, Louisiana; The Chester County Historical Society, West Chester, Pennsylvania; Independence National Historical Park, Philadelphia; The Mint Museum, Charlotte, North Carolina; The Museum of Art, Rhode Island School of Design, Providence, Rhode Island; The Nantucket Historical Association, Nantucket, Massachusetts; The New Jersey State Museum, Trenton, New Jersey; Old Salem, Inc., Winston-Salem, North Carolina; The Peabody Museum, Salem, Massachusetts; The State Museum of Pennsylvania, Harrisburg, Pennsylvania; Waynesburg College, Waynesburg, Pennsylvania; and the Henry du Pont Winterthur Museum, Winterthur, Delaware.

Among the private and corporate collectors who graciously allowed me to borrow or photograph objects for the book and exhibit, I wish to thank Meryle Evans of New York City; Joseph Felcone of Princeton, New Jersey; Mr. and Mrs. James Gergat of Avondale, Pennsylvania; Mr. and Mrs. Kent Gilyard of Bantam, Connecticut; Pat Guthman of Southport, Connecticut; IBM Corporation of Armonk, New York; Mr. and Mrs. Alton Long of Strafford, Pennsylvania; Hazel Marcus of Union, Maine; Alice Ross of Smithtown, New York; Chandler Saint of Milford, Pennsylvania; Quincy Scarborough of Fayetteville, North Carolina; and Dr. James F. Turk of Mullica Hill, New Jersey.

Then there is a special handful of individuals who volunteered their time, their thoughts, and generous advice, all of which made my research less tedious and far richer than I ever imagined possible. Among these I want to give particular thanks to ceramic specialists Ralph Bloom of the Norwalk Museum, Norwalk, Connecticut; Ellen Denker of Wilmington, Delaware; and Eva Mounce of the Foundation for Historical Research of Illinois Potteries, Streator, Illinois. I would also like to thank Donald H. Davis of Zion Grove, Pennsylvania; Annajane Heddesheimer of Valley Forge, Pennsylvania; and Lisa and Barry McAllister of Clear Spring, Maryland, dealers whose vigilance brought to light some of the unusual culinary objects illustrated in this book.

A word too must be said for Henry Glassie, recently of the University of Pennsylvania, now of Indiana University. Henry and I spin in very different orbits—his being academia, mine being "out there"—but now and then the tails of our comets have touched. The jolt has always opened my mental eyes a little wider. I think Henry will be pleased to see that I have molded an exhibit—and book—around a part of his doctoral dissertation, which may be a measure of how many steps behind him I still walk. My creation may also surprise him, and I thank him heartily for letting me use his map to help prove my case.

Ellen Slack, poet laureate of Bucks County, Pennsylvania, friend, kindred spirit, and cataloguer of Lewis Mumford's papers, certainly must be thanked for discovering the rare Mumford quote about food, just as *The New Republic* must be thanked for granting permission to cite it. Also, Werner Janney and Asa Moore Janney must be thanked for permission to cite a few lines from their excellent little book *John Jay Janney's Virginia*.

Finally, the staff of the Museum of American Folk Art deserves a special word of thanks for standing by me and my difficult assignment. A folk food exhibit for an art museum was certainly an untested experiment. Robert Bishop, director of the museum, had the vision long ago to give this unusual project his blessing. Elizabeth Warren, curator of the museum, respected my judgment in ways all too rare in the museum world, and I deeply appreciate it. Michael McManus, director of exhibitions, did his best to eat samples and keep the guest curator in good spirits, on time and on target.

Everyone involved in this effort is grateful to my editor, Susan Friedland, whose personal commitment and monumental persuasiveness got us past seemingly impossible obstacles, and in no time at all, we had a book.

AMERICA EATS
FORMS OF EDIBLE FOLK ART

From *The Peasant's Repast* (Philadelphia, 1808).
(Roughwood Collection)

1

AMERICA EATS:
FORMS · OF · EDIBLE · FOLK · ART

The Peasant's Repast

One has only to read the traveler's notes on country hotels up to 1850,
to realize that in the more civil parts of the country the person who
referred to the "bounty of nature" had literally said a mouthful.
Indeed, in various parts of New England today, if one is careful to dodge
the Dew-Drop Inns, and urban deceptions of a similar nature,
one can still come upon country breakfasts and dinners that have the
ancient charm of elementary good cooking: one does not select from their
bills of fare: the food rather advances in waves, and it is a scant and
unfriendly dinner that has less than four vegetables and three meat dishes.
New England cooking, it is true, like its prototype across the ocean,
is a kind of cooking which relies far more upon content than upon
a subtle technique: but the point is, when a chicken has not been
exposed to arctic hardships, when the beef is something more than the
left-overs of the glue factory and the button mill, and when the
beans or peas or corn have not been tanned and desiccated in the process
of going to market, anything more than plain cooking is mere gilt on the lily.

—Lewis Mumford, "Back to the Table," *The New Republic*, August 15, 1928

When Lewis Mumford wrote this more than sixty years ago, he meant to call attention to a cookery, an "elementary good cooking," that was still firmly rooted in its old New England past. For Mumford, it was a cookery characterized by its adroitness with things simple and its honesty of content. He was judging it by artistic standards, standards of excellence quite similar, in fact, to those by which he judged architecture.

Architecture is ordered by structure, and so too is cookery: by structure of content, its organic composition, and by structure of form, the organization of its physical and most visible parts. Form is further articulated by decoration—or by a conscious lack of it.

When Elizabeth Lea, in her *Domestic Cookery* of 1851, placed her Mansfield muffins in tin rings, she was ordering their physical form to conform to a preconceived idea of shape.[1] When she spread her johnny cake on a board before the fire, smoothed it over with a wet hand, and then scored it with a knife, she was imposing decorative pattern upon form.[2] In the act of scoring, which was necessary to prevent the cake surface from blistering, Elizabeth Lea may have discovered a variety of pattern arrangements that pleased her eye. This may have encouraged her to experiment, to give vent to the aesthetic inclinations implied in her recipe for preserving green lemons: "Cut them in such shapes as you please."[3] It is possible to find similar hints and passing allusions to the artistic side of American folk cookery scattered throughout early American culinary literature.

The meaning of the term *folk cookery* is as fluid as the meaning of *haute cuisine*. It is a label that changes with time; thus, we are constantly called upon to redefine it, to pinpoint its shifts and new associations. The *haute cuisine* of eighteenth-century France is not the fashionable cookery of the modern Paris restaurant. The folk cookery of eighteenth-century Virginia is not the food of the day laborer in modern Richmond.

In folk art, there is no fixed or universally accepted definition of what is meant by *folk*. But folk cookery, at least, can be defined according to its context. "Classical" folk cookery of early America may be described largely in terms of its agrarian character and its "connectedness."

When I interviewed Alice Ross (a professional hearth cook) for an article about early American cooking practices in the *New York Times,* we discussed the meaning of *connectedness.*[4] We both agreed that it was not an easy subject to elucidate because it involved several levels of meaning at the same time. It is also highly charged with deeply rooted emotional associations.

In early American folk cookery, pre–Civil War folk cookery, connectedness was a bond with the community that radiated outward from the cook through her children, through kinfolk, and through the man who had placed her at the center of his little world. It was the interaction of people caring for one another through food. One form of this was hog butchering, when families gathered to help each other prepare meat and sausage for the winter.

Connectedness was also a direct association with place, what the Swiss call *Talschaft* (literally "valleyness"): the valley and its community. The people of the Mahantongo Valley in eastern Pennsylvania, known in the folk-art world for their ornately painted furniture, cultivate to this day a keen sense of *Talschaft,* of belonging to a particular place and to each other. Such identities are also strong in Appalachia and other regions where Americans established early cultural patterns.

The funeral biscuit, discussed in chapter 4, was one means of cementing this connection between community and its landscape. These biscuits, saved from one funeral to the next, served as reminders of particular individuals, just as the rows of headstones in the churchyard, decorated with similar motifs, reminded all who passed of the "story" of each person buried there.

Connectedness also meant a direct tie to one's natural surroundings: the woods, the pastures, the streams. Each of these had a particular sanctity, but none was more important than the kitchen garden. The cook, who stood among her cabbages in her bare feet, was mistress of her own food supply. She watched her corn as it grew; she helped the milch cow when it was in labor. She knew the right time to pick peaches so that they would caramelize in the fullness of their own natural sugar when she fried them in a skillet. Or, with lap churn in hand, she knew when to sing a little melody to help the butter come. She knew the weather—she *felt* it. She knew which hillsides had the best mountain blueberries and which pastures had the best morels each spring. This is the connectedness that California restaurateur Alice Waters has tried to restore, in an intellectualized way, to contemporary American cookery.

Folk cookery changes when any one of these threads of connectedness is broken. The Italian farmer who leaves rural Calabria for New York gives up his connectedness and replaces it with a cultural memory we call *ethnicity.* The Appalachian farmer who migrates to Pittsburgh to work in the mills gives up his connectedness in exchange for a similar remembered identity. In an urban setting, each group, old American or new, is as "ethnic" as the other, since each is carrying with it its own cultural baggage.

Ethnicity has become an urban American replacement for lost connectedness. It has created its own web of ties, its own food symbols, and its own sense of *Talschaft* through the neighborhood church, a grocery store, or through a restaurant that touches base with foods and menus remembered from another place. This kind of folk cookery survives out of its original context because it is portable, like ethnicity. But over time, unless it is fortified by religious belief or continuously replenished from the outside with new individuals, it eventually shrinks and fades into the culture of the suburbs. There, it is sometimes revived in the form of selective ethnicity—a rediscovered and selectively relearned identity—or transformed into an aesthetic statement, as in "country style" cookbooks, dining rooms hung with quilts, or kitchens decorated with folk pottery.

Folk cookery is also sometimes called *traditional cookery,* just as folk art is sometimes called *traditional art.* At times, writers use *traditional* interchangeably with *folk;* at other times, they use it to avoid the connotation of *peasant,* taboo word that it is, which is always lurking behind any American discussion of folk culture.

Since the United States experienced a revival of interest in colonial taste and style after the 1870s, the distinctions between colonial high cookery, folk cookery, and middle-class fare were quickly, and I might add, naively, blurred. Now that this revival is itself a century old, we of the 1980s are often presented with a skewed vision of life before the Civil War. This has not made the study of our folk culture any easier.

Batter pot by the Morgan Pottery, Cheesequake, New Jersey, circa 1775. (Philadelphia Museum of Art)

In 1859 Caroline Gilman described the cookery of her mother:

Her sausages were pronounced to be the best flavored in the neighborhood; her hog's cheese (the English brawn) was delicacy itself; her curds, made in a heart-mould, covered with nutmeg and cream, won the hearts of many a guest; her clabber was turned at that precise moment when a slight acidity tempers the insipidity of milk; her wafers bore the prettiest devices, or were rolled in the thinnest possible consistency; her shrimps, pickled or fresh, were most carefully prepared; her preserved water-melons were carved with the taste of a sculptor; her hominy looked like plates of gathered snow; corn and rice lent all their nice varieties to her breakfast; and her boiled rice answered Shakespeare's description, for "each particular *grain* did stand on end," or to use a more expressive term, crawled.[5]

These are the makings of the sort of folk cookery Lewis Mumford so greatly admired, a cookery that was truly an art. On the other hand, this was dining at Roseland Plantation in South Carolina, no hovel. I think it would be fair to say that in spite of the rice that crawled (or because of it), this was certainly cookery on the upper end of "folk."

It is therefore important to keep in mind that early American folk cookery not only embraced connectedness, it also displayed definite economic divisions and different levels of accomplishment. In fact, quality of food and type of cookery was much more a sign of class in the nineteenth century than it is today.

At the other end of folk cookery, the end opposite Roseland Plantation, was the drab world that Mrs. Gilman knew about but rarely mingled with. It was the world of servants and slaves. Servants were often the culinary links between two social worlds because they were "bilingual" in palate. They cooked in two styles, one for Mistress and one for themselves. Mrs. Gilman recalled that hoppin john was a "good dish, to be sure, but no more presentable to strangers at the South than baked beans and pork in New-England."[6]

Hoppin john, a rice-and-bean dish that is now a metaphor for South Carolina cookery, was not at that time respectable. Family might eat it if necessity demanded, maids certainly ate it, but *never* company. How could such fare eventually acquire the trappings of a state symbol? How could it cut across class and custom, even race? Perhaps part of the answer lies in the fact that for South Carolinians, hoppin john symbolizes connectedness, their sense of community and place. It is not just food.

Glance around the country and similar dishes come to mind: catfish soup along the

Mississippi River, cracker hash in Indiana and Illinois, *Schnitz-un-Gnepp* among the Pennsylvania Dutch. Stepping back in time, into the early nineteenth century, there were other dishes, now mostly forgotten, that in their own day symbolized a culture and place: venison ham from Virginia's Eastern Shore—a rare delicacy served like chipped beef;[7] the fish chowders of Nantucket; Connecticut corn pudding, a kind of fresh-corn spoon bread;[8] and buckwheat cakes for winter breakfast in the region stretching from northern Virginia to Long Island. Potteries in the "buckwheat belt," especially in New Jersey and Pennsylvania, churned out thousands of stoneware batter pots for this purpose. Virginian John Janney wrote about them when describing his mother's Loudoun County kitchen in the 1820s:

> At night the "batter pot" was set near the fire to keep warm, and sometimes the batter would become too light. It was not an uncommon thing to find a good deal of the batter run over the hearth in the morning, and some crickets in the batter. Crickets were common in all kitchens.[9]

The simplicity of such fare—deceptively simple when cooked to perfection—calls to mind the description of an 1860s dinner published in *Aunt Betsy's Rule,* a book whose purpose was to instruct children how *not* to behave:

> The meat was placed in the middle of a platter, and the potatoes in a circle round the rim, and the other vegetables in heaps at each corner. If they had a pudding or a pandowdy, it was set on at the same time. There was but one set of knives and forks to put on, and each one helped himself with his own knife and fork, sticking his fork into the piece of meat on the platter, and cutting off a slice with the knife he used in eating. In the same way, a piece of bread or butter was cut, and the tip of the knife dipped in the salt.
>
> The pitcher of water was passed round the table, and all drank from it. After the meat was eaten, or at the same time, if any one chose, he would help himself to pudding, piling everything on the same plate.[10]

A comparison of this meal with the table at Roseland Plantation should point to some of the differences between the varying degrees of "folk." In fact, the rustic feast just described has a parallel in an old custom of serving venison, mentioned in passing by Sarah J. Hale in her 1848 edition of Eliza Acton's *Modern Cookery*.[11]

Country people in the Middle Colonies during the 1600s and early 1700s ate plain venison roasts with minced shallots or Catawissa onions, or even bulbs of wild garlic; this in conjunction with sweet or sharp sauces, such as pepper dram or man-dram, a mixture of chopped cucumbers or West India gherkins and pepper vinegar.

Pepper vinegar was also put into pea and bean soups. It can be made with little dif-ficulty by placing a few pods of cayenne in a bottle with one part sherry to three parts white vinegar, preferably white-wine vin-egar. Some people also added a few allspice berries. But as Mrs. Hale pointed out, none of this was found "at refined tables."

Schnitz-un-Gnepp: An Example of Tradition and Continuity

As in folk art, tradition in folk cookery *is* continuity. Tradition in the classic Euro-pean sense of folk cookery is perhaps best illustrated in *Schnitz-un-Gnepp,* the Penn-sylvania Dutch stew shown on the cover of this book. *Schnitz-un-Gnepp* is Penn-sylvania Dutch dialect for "sliced dried ap-ples and dumplings." If we were to place it on an evolutionary chart, we would put it among the more recent lineal descendants of *Gumbis.*

Gumbis is a Pennsylvania Dutch dialect term; it has no precise equivalent in En-glish. In his recipe for the dish, which may be found at the end of this chapter, George Girardey called it *Kumbish,* his own pecu-liar spelling. Girardey's 1842 recipe is the earliest known version of Gumbis pub-lished in this country. Older recipes exist in manuscript form but often under a vari-ety of other names.

The word *Gumbis* is a corruption of the Latin *compositum,* a term used in the Mid-dle Ages for certain "compositions" or dishes of mixed ingredients usually ar-ranged in layers.[12] *Composita* were divided into two groups—vertical and horizontal; that is, preparations that required tall, nar-row pots and those that required broad, or shallow ones. The basic implements, as they were known since the late Middle Ages, were illustrated in Michael Hero's *Schachtafeln der Gesundheit* ("Chessboard of Health"), printed at Strassburg in 1533. Those woodcuts, by Hero's illustrator Hans Weiditz, are reproduced here.

Gumbis was usually prepared in the broad, three-footed redware pots which, by the late eighteenth century, were generally replaced in Pennsylvania by cast-iron utensils. But several potteries continued to make the traditional, tall "stewpots" into the 1880s. Willoughby Smith of Womelsdorf, Berks County, is probably the best known of these among redware collectors today.

As it was known to the early settlers of southeastern Pennsylvania, Gumbis was a dish composed of layers of cabbage, apples, and meat, usually gammon (either slab bacon or ham hock). The apples could be dried or fresh. In fact, the variables were almost infinite, from venison Gumbis made with cabbage, sliced pears, and peach Schnitz, to veal Gumbis made with prunes. George W. Huntley, in his reminiscences of lumbering in Cameron County, Pennsylvania, recorded a version of Gumbis made with layers of "flitch" (unsmoked slab bacon in Pennsylvania parlance), onions, and sauerkraut.[13] The *Vollständiges Nürnbergisches Koch-Buch* (Complete Nürnberg Cookbook) of 1691 included a recipe for *Kumpus-Kraut,* a Gumbis composed of layers of young cabbage leaves, kale, bread-crumbs, bits of lard, and caraway seeds.[14] The beauty of any Gumbis recipe is its adaptability. One can leave out or add ingredients as one wishes, as long as the basic composition maintains its layered cabbage character. In this health-conscious age, it is one of the easiest ways to create an interesting one-pot meal out of inexpensive, low-calorie ingredients.

Recipes for *Schnitz-un-Gnepp* are found in almost every cookbook claiming to be Pennsylvania Dutch. The name does not imply the presence of meat, although most Pennsylvania German cooks add ham or at least part of a ham hock. Technically speaking, *Schnitz-un-Gnepp* should be meatless, since in Europe it was originally a Lenten dish, with flour dumplings taking the place of meat. Dumplings and dried fruit, usually apples, were placed in layers in the pot and covered with hot water. The advantage in the tall shape of the pot was that the heat would penetrate evenly and in a relatively short time from all sides, and only a very small surface area of food (at the top) would be exposed to smoke and falling ash when the lid was removed. In traditional folk cookery, the flavor of cooking smoke was generally viewed as a sign of bad technique.

Iron pot pushers helped the cook move the pot around on the hearth (old German and Pennsylvania German hearths were raised above floor level), and a special iron hook with a long wooden handle was called into action if the pot was too far back in the fire to pull out by hand. The

hook went through the loop of the handle, and old pots that have managed to survive the rough use of time often show considerable wear about their handles and bases, both from the hook and from repeated dragging of the pot across the hot hearth surface.[15] In spite of the fact that these cookpots show hearth wear and charring on the bottom, they are all too often accessioned by museums in this country as chamber pots, which calls to mind a Pennsylvania Dutch joke that I could never repeat here.

The Pennsylvania Germans do not seem to have developed uniform dialect terms for any of these pots, perhaps because the pots themselves were put to a wide variety of uses, but also perhaps because the Pennsylvania Germans themselves were a mixture of immigrant groups from many different parts of German-speaking Europe. And by the time their culture had coalesced into something essentially American by the early nineteenth century, many of the older folk dishes had already fallen out of fashion.

The French, however, call the tall, narrow pot a *cassoulet,* after the traditional clay cooking pot or *cassol* of Issel near Castelnaudary in the department of Aude. In fact, the cassoulet was made in many parts of France and Europe (and North Africa) in the Middle Ages and was known by a

BACON & GREENS.

As sung by Robt. H. Craig, Esq., of the Arch Street Theatre.

I have lived long enough to be rarely mistaken,
    And had my full share of life's changeable scenes ;
But my woes have been solaced by good greens and bacon,
    My joys have been doubled by bacon and greens.
What a thrill of remembrance e'en now they awaken,
    Of childhood's gay morning and youth's merry scenes ;
When one day we had greens and a plateful of bacon,
    And the next we had bacon and a plateful of greens.

Ah ! well I remember, when sad and forsaken,
    Heart-wrung by the scorn of a miss in her teens,
How I fled from her sight to my loved greens and bacon,
    And forgot my despair over bacon and greens.
When the banks refused specie, and credit was shaken,
    I shared in the wreck, and was ruined in means ;
My friends all declared I had not saved my bacon,
    But I lived, for I still had my bacon and greens.

If some fairy a grant of three wishes could make one
    So worthless as I, and so laden with sins,
I'd wish all the greens in the world, then the bacon,
    Then wish for a little more bacon and greens.
Oh ! there is a charm in this dish, rightly taken,
    Which from custards and jellies an epicure weans ;
Stick your fork in the fat ; wrap your greens round the bacon,
    And you'll vow there's no dish like good bacon and greens.

Philadelphia street ballad from the Civil War period celebrating a popular American folk dish. (Roughwood Collection)

variety of local names. Suffice it to say, if we look at Roman cooking pots, it becomes suddenly clear that we are dealing with a family of folk dishes of truly ancient origin. Folk cookery, like folk architecture, is not the product of ethnicity but rather part of a group's acquired cultural trappings, just as hoppin john has become a symbol of something intangible, something South Carolinian.[16] The divergent articulation of ingredients over time is the result of differences in climate, food supply, and historical experience.

In every case, there is a direct relationship between the pot, its functional form, and the preparation made in it. Culinary objects must be viewed as only half of a duality, half of a process. Stew and pot are like yin and yang.

The Origins of America Eats

Similar—and quite elaborate—family histories could be compiled for many American folk dishes, from Boston baked beans to New Orleans *gâteau du roi,* the festive cake eaten from Twelfth Night (January 6) to Mardi Gras. But studies of this sort are still relatively new to American cultural research, leaving aside, of course, the vast slag heaps of journalistic lore that have accumulated in newspapers and magazines since the nineteenth century.

American folklore assumed the lead many years ago in taking up the pen for American foods and foodways (mostly the latter). In general, however, American folklore does not deal with material culture but rather with the verbal culture of the present. It analyzes immediacy and impression largely disconnected from the past, and in this respect there is an ephemeral quality to the science.

Here and there, however, individuals have surfaced who took a deeper interest in the complexities of food, among them John Gregory Bourke and his pioneering study of the folk foods of the Rio Grande Valley in 1895; Atwater and Woods, who published a dietary survey of the Negro in Alabama in 1897; and Hans Kurath, whose six-volume *Linguistic Atlas of New England* (1939–43) contains extraordinary quantities of information on food terms such as *johnny cake,* the *crambury* of Cape Cod, and *bonny clabber* (sour milk as thick as junket) from the coast of Maine.[17]

Kurath's wide-ranging surveys, taken on a township-by-township basis, did much to pinpoint certain food terms to particular localities, but in asking people if they knew the term *johnny cake,* he did not ask them what they *meant* by it—that is, what sort of recipe they used. Very important information about regional variations, such as differences in cornmeal or preparation techniques, were therefore never recorded.

The recipe is crucial to any study of cookery because it is an indicator of structure, a blueprint if you will. Without a recipe for New England apple pandowdy —the dessert mentioned in the rustic dinner described earlier—it is impossible to know that it is the same thing as brown betty in the South.[18]

In 1938 the U.S. government mobilized a grass-roots survey called the Federal Foodways Research Program to tackle the broad issues of American food customs. It was one of those Depression-spawned WPA projects designed to create work for unemployed writers and journalists. Individuals in forty-two states were organized into teams to collect materials on their respective regional foodways.

This material was to be sifted and distilled into a monumental book entitled *America Eats*. These noble intentions, unfortunately, never materialized. The convoluted history of how *America Eats* began and ended has been analyzed by Charles Camp in his 1978 doctoral dissertation for the University of Pennsylvania.[19] I have borrowed the title of the old WPA project for my exhibit and this book, because my own goals are to some extent similar. Furthermore, the first *America Eats* was a historic experiment that deserves greater recognition in American food history.

The war emergency brought the project to an abrupt end in 1942, and the large archive of material assembled for the book was eventually put to pasture in a warehouse in Alexandria, Virginia. Eventually, the Library of Congress acquired jurisdiction over most of the papers and has now taken charge of their care.

The work of the WPA teams did not go unnoticed by writers outside the project, and it surprised no one that a number of books with a similar focus surfaced at the height of research activity. The two most important were Richard Cummings's *The American and His Food,* issued by the University of Chicago Press in 1940; and the Cora, Rose, and Bob Brown cookbook entitled *America Cooks,* published by W. W. Norton that same year. Both works drew in varying degrees on material from the America Eats project. This effectively limited publication possibilities for an America Eats book, which formally took shape in 1941.

Nowhere in the America Eats project or in any of the spin-off books was there a serious discussion of food in terms of material culture. Apocryphal material such as "The Discovery of Maple Syrup," "The Origin of the Popcorn Ball," and "The Origin of Hush Puppies," much of which is traceable to copy on commercial food packaging, interested the food buffs in the field more than issues like the cook as folk artist, or user of folk implements; or the complex relationship of cook to implement and implement to food; or even the web of links that gave rural cooks in the 1930s their personal sense of connectedness.

Many years later Henry Glassie brought a useful overview to folklife research with his *Pattern in the Material Folk Culture of the Eastern United States* (University of Pennsylvania Press, 1968). It is a long title for a book that both pioneered new ideas and served as his doctoral dissertation—a rare and happy combination.

Glassie found that American regional cultures evolved in small, limited areas of early settlement along the Atlantic Seaboard. He called these settlement areas *culture hearths,* since they were the "warm spots" on the map where the various "yeasts" of Old World folk culture rapidly hybridized to form something new and uniquely American. His list of hearths included southern New England (particularly Connecticut), southeastern Pennsylvania, the Chesapeake Bay area (both the Virginia and Maryland sides), the coastal Carolinas, and Georgia. There is also one that he did not mention: the Cajun area of Lower Louisiana. In these different regions, Americans evolved distinctive ways of doing things, distinctive vocabularies in language, and distinctive traits in architecture—like the New England saltbox and a host of objects designed along regional or highly localized lines.

Among the objects that Glassie classified were slat-back chairs, barns, gravestones, eel spears, and corn knives. Though he did not deal with parallels in food, it is possible to take Glassie's models and match up his chairs with regional differences in setting tables—or seating order around the tables —his barns with regional differences in storing grain, his gravestones with different forms of funeral biscuits, his eel spears with regional ways of collaring eel (pickling it in aspic), and his corn knives with regional and localized types of "bread corn"—yellow cornmeal in New England, white in the South, parched in the Middle States. In essence, the rules that Glassie established for folk objects also apply to folk foods.

As Americans moved out of these regional settlement areas, they took their distinctive regional cultures with them and spread their folkways over a greater area of the United States. The basic patterns that molded American foods and eating habits as we know them today—Thanksgiving dinner, barbecued meats, milk on breakfast cereals, the hot dog, coffee drinking—evolved in these coastal settlement areas.

That is why this book concentrates on the eastern half of the country. Glassie's map of the major cultural regions east of the Mississippi River also outlines the major divisions in American folk cookery. There are distinctive "styles" of cooking and food preparation in each region.

Before the Civil War and the advent of industrialized meat packing, there were regional differences in butchering, carving, and preserving cuts of meat. Hams from

Map of the five major regional folk cultures of the eastern United States. Reproduced with the permission of Henry Glassie.

Burlington, New Jersey, were once considered among the best in the colonies, and their peculiar delicacy added great character to local parsnip dishes dressed with mustard.

Butter in New York and New England was more heavily salted and put up differently from butter in New Jersey, Pennsylvania, and Delaware. It therefore required washing and squeezing before it could be used in pastry or cakes.[20] Recipes from New York and New England often mention this procedure and can be identified by it, even when no source is given.

In Appalachia, where milch cows were few and butter making was done on a very small scale, lap churns and lap troughs were more common than in other parts of the country. The butter was worked by hand with a "clasher," from which the folk expression "clash," meaning "to gossip," is derived.[21] One could presumably clash both butter and the neighbors at the same time.

The form of the Appalachian lap trough was taken over from Native American culture; it was originally the work bowl Indian women used for making bread.[22] Generally speaking, however, white culture did not respond to Indian foodways. The Indian was more of a decorative motif in folk art than an equal partner in culinary exchange, in spite of the long list of vegetables Europeans took over from the Indian

Mohawk bread paddle from the Upper Hudson Valley.

Gingerbread stamp depicting a stylized King Phillip, a famous New England Indian chief, circa 1820. (Old Sturbridge Village)

Appalachian "clasher" and lap trough.

diet. Many wild vegetables, such as cattails (the spikes were the part used), were eaten only as emergency foods by whites; or like ramps (a wild onion), they were eaten only in areas of extreme poverty, as in Appalachia.[23] Even in a dish like corn drop dumplings, which resemble dumplings made by Native Americans, the structural composition (particularly the egg and the wheat flour) and the technique for boiling them are taken directly from European cookery.

The recipe that I have included at the end of this chapter was perfected by a chef in a Louisville, Kentucky, hotel. Today, the recipe often appears in American Indian cookbooks.

More interesting are the European influences on the Indians themselves, a process of acculturation that also varied from region to region and tribe to tribe. Among the Mohawks of the Upper Hudson Valley, European iron-making techniques were learned and adjusted to local requirements, as in the case of iron bread paddles (used for stirring cornmeal), which retained the form and decorative motifs of their carved wooden antecedents.[24]

All of Henry Glassie's five cultural regions produced products or goods that were used in commerce with other parts of the country, so that to a degree, the material culture of the eastern United States, while regionalized, was also highly mixed. This was particularly true around port towns.

For example, because of an abundance of good clay and proximity to transportation routes, southeastern Pennsylvania became a center for the production of redware pottery—especially pie plates.[25] This pottery often traveled many hundreds of miles along river trade networks or overland down the Great Road into the valley of Virginia and Tennessee.[26]

North Carolina developed a thriving industry in salt-glazed stoneware in the early nineteenth century. Salt-glazed wares were essential to home cookery for pickling and for food preservation because the glazing did not react with acids. For this reason, there was always a large demand for such stoneware, at least until the appearance of glass canning jars in the 1850s and 1860s.

Local clay deposits in North Carolina that had gone undeveloped in the eigh- teenth century for lack of potters were effectively exploited in the nineteenth century in an attempt to undercut the cost of wares shipped south from New Jersey, New York, and Connecticut. Yet many of the potters who set up shop in North Carolina came from Connecticut and brought with them Connecticut techniques of pottery decoration. Thus, some North Carolina stoneware has a noticeable affinity with older Connecticut forms. This is especially true of the Webster School of potters in Fayetteville.[27]

Likewise, food moved across regional boundaries. The *Wilmington Chronicle* of Wilmington, North Carolina, advertised in its October 1, 1795, edition that a large shipment of cheese, butter, and onions from New Haven, Connecticut, was available for sale. Onions, which could be raised in the poor soil along the Connecticut coast, were one of the state's major export products. Later, by the mid-nineteenth century, Connecticut also became a center of commercial basket making because it was centrally located to the farms then supplying fruit to Boston and New York by railroad. Since the baskets could be produced cheaply by machine and shipped by train to truck farms all along the East Coast, the Connecticut factories effectively put an end to the older cottage basket industry in New Jersey.[28]

From an 1881 wood engraving.

OPPOSITE PAGE: New Jersey berry basket by Ebenezer Thompson, dated February 25, 1852.

Even in the early eighteenth century, the handmade New Jersey berry basket was a common feature in East Coast markets—and highly regarded for its craftsmanship. The baskets were usually small, with five to seven holding a quart. They were made by fruit growers or by rural families over the winter. One household might produce several thousand in one season.[29] The baskets were made for transporting strawberries, raspberries, blueberries, cranberries, and other small fruit to market. There, the fruit would be emptied into wooden trays and the baskets discarded or sold to customers. In an age before brown shopping bags, customers were expected to bring their own containers to market.

In terms of cookery, recipes and ideas moved as readily as Connecticut onions. On Long Island, for example, there developed in the seventeenth century a particularly successful technique for making a "ferment" or sourdough yeast from apples or pumpkins. Doubtless for many years the recipe was traded orally through neighborhood networks, then published in regional newspapers and almanacs. Finally, in 1819, when it was already an heirloom, it appeared in *The New Family Receipt Book,* printed at New Haven, a book that was distributed far beyond the borders of Lower New England—my copy, in fact, belonged to a Mrs. Baker of Augusta,

Georgia. Bread made off island using this ferment for a leaven was sometimes called "Long Island Bread," even though none of the ingredients in it actually came from the island.

The colloquial nature of terminology in folk cookery is both its joy and its undoing. Because vast confusions can arise over differences real or perceived, it is usually necessary to collate the recipes, as in the case of the New England apple pandowdy or brown betty already mentioned.

In the case of objects, pictures are worth at least a hundred recipes. Otherwise, who would ever guess that the oystermen of Philadelphia, New York, and Boston used oyster knives of such unusual and varied shapes? The knives pictured here have been commercially produced; in effect, industrialization has imitated a pre-existing folk form. The New Jersey oystermen, however, developed a knife form of their own. Consisting of a small axlike blade mounted to a block of wood, it was never committed to the drawing boards of a manufacturer. It now ranks among the rarest (and most lethal!) of American oyster-knife forms.

All of these varying patterns, whether berry basket, yeast recipe, or commercial oyster knife, imply an even greater complexity of affairs when dealing with the subject of food, particularly cookery as an art form. Art takes its cue from nature, and the connectedness of the folk cook with her natural surroundings is nowhere more evident than in the productions of her kitchen. With these, she invites new sensations of taste and smell and leads the imagination to discovery. In the folk logic of Appalachia, hers is the instinctive understanding that the eye eats first.

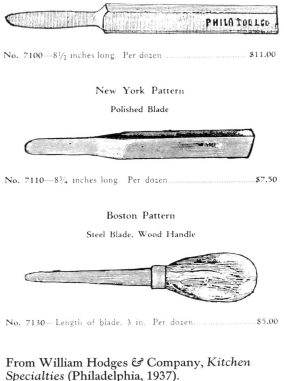

STEEL OYSTER KNIVES
Philadelphia Pattern
Polished Blade

No. 7100—8½ inches long. Per dozen........................$11.00

New York Pattern
Polished Blade

No. 7110—8¾ inches long. Per dozen.......................$7.50

Boston Pattern
Steel Blade. Wood Handle

No. 7130— Length of blade. 3 in. Per dozen...................$5.00

From William Hodges & Company, *Kitchen Specialties* (Philadelphia, 1937). (Roughwood Collection)

CATFISH SOUP

1903

YIELD: 6 TO 8 SERVINGS.

1 pound boned fillet of catfish
½ pound slab bacon, diced
½ large onion (4 ounces), sliced
2 quarts water
¼ cup minced parsley
Salt and pepper to taste

THICKENER:

1½ teaspoons unsalted butter
1 tablespoon all-purpose flour
2 egg yolks
½ cup milk (at room temperature)

Cut the fish into large chunks. Fry the bacon in a stewing pan until it begins to brown, then add the onion. Stir-fry to wilt the onion, then add the water. Boil gently for 15 minutes, skim off foam from the top, and add the parsley.

Thicken as follows: Work the butter and flour to a paste. Beat the egg yolks and combine with the paste, then add the milk and whisk smooth. Pour this into the broth, whisking as you pour so that it does not form lumps. Then add the fish. Simmer for about 15 minutes, or until the fish is cooked through but not falling apart.

NOTE:

This will remind many people of oyster stew. Old-timers like to add broken oyster crackers, which gives the soup additional character.

SOURCE: Frances E. Owens. *Mrs. Owens's Cook Book and Useful Household Hints.* (Chicago: American Publishing House, 1903), 15–16.

CORN DROP DUMPLINGS
1897

This is the recipe of Eugene Stuyvesant Howard, who was chef de cuisine of the Louisville Hotel in Louisville, Kentucky, during the 1890s. YIELD: 4 SERVINGS.

1¾ cups freshly grated corn
(see note)
2 eggs
⅓ cup all-purpose flour
¼ teaspoon salt

¼ teaspoon white pepper
1 tablespoon minced parsley
(optional)
Sugar (optional)

Run corn through a meat grinder or puree in a food processor to batter consistency. Beat the eggs to a froth, then beat them into the corn. Sift in the flour and add the seasonings. You may add minced parsley if you choose, and if the corn is not flavorful, a little sugar may enhance it.

Bring a deep kettle of salted water to a hard boil, then lower the heat to a gentle boil. Drop the batter from a measuring teaspoon into the water and let the dumplings cook until they rise to the top. The dumplings will expand to about the size of a quarter; they will become heavy if they are overcooked.

NOTE:
Yield will vary depending on the type of corn used. For the 1¾ cups pureed corn needed here, allow about 4 to 5 medium ears of corn.

SOURCE: *Standard American Cook Book.* (Springfield: Crowell & Kirkpatrick, 1897), 85.

FRIED PEACHES

1885

YIELD: 4 TO 8 SERVINGS.

4 ripe peaches
2 tablespoons lard or lightly salted butter

4 teaspoons white sugar
Cinnamon (optional)

Pare and halve the peaches. Discard the pits. Heat the lard or butter until it is foaming hot, then lay the peaches pit-side down in the pan. Fry until the peaches turn golden brown, then turn them over and fill each cavity with ½ teaspoon sugar. Continue to fry until the peaches are fully cooked. Serve immediately as a side dish with ham and grits, or as a dessert with vanilla ice cream.

NOTE:

Many cooks in the rural South used ham or pork drippings instead of lard or butter. Cinnamon was sometimes mixed with the sugar. If the peaches are not sweet, this will greatly improve them.

SOURCE: Mrs. E. R. Tennent. *House-Keeping in the Sunny South.* (Atlanta, Ga.: James P. Harrison & Co., 1885), 82.

Afro-American coil baskets, Charleston, South Carolina.

CRACKER HASH
1884

Nellie-Mae White, my Indiana-born "white gravy" grandmother (and daughter of one of the founders of the Indiana W.C.T.U.), could not have cracker hash without the best part: fried tomato gravy.

Since white gravies are still a feature of typical menus in this region of the country, I have appended a recipe Nellie-Mae would approve of.[30] YIELD: 6 SERVINGS.

1 pound ground beef
1½ cups boiling water
⅔ cup cracker crumbs
½ teaspoon salt

¼ teaspoon fresh black pepper
2 tablespoons cold, lightly salted butter, chopped

Preheat the oven to 350°F.

Put the meat in a stewing pan and pour the boiling water over it. Cook 5 minutes, then add the cracker crumbs, salt, and pepper. Mix thoroughly and pour into a shallow earthenware baking dish about 10 inches in diameter. If too dry, moisten slightly with more water (see note). Smooth the surface of the batter and dot with the chopped cold butter. Bake in the preheated oven for 35 to 45 minutes, or until brown. Serve from the baking dish with fried tomato gravy. Boiled potatoes make a perfect side dish.

NOTE:
Cracker hash can be made in a number of ways. Some like it very loose and moist, others like it thick and dry. This recipe is about midway between. It should cut with a knife and lift out like a slice of pie.

FRIED TOMATO GRAVY

YIELD: SUFFICIENT GRAVY FOR 6 SERVINGS.

2 tablespoons lard or lightly
salted butter
1 large ripe tomato
(8 ounces), sliced
2 tablespoons minced onion
or shallot

2 teaspoons all-purpose flour
½ cup hot cream
2 teaspoons chopped parsley
Salt and pepper

Heat a heavy iron skillet and melt the lard. When the lard is very hot, add the tomatoes and fry until they begin to soften. Add the onion or shallot and fry another 2 to 3 minutes. Then sprinkle in the flour and let it absorb most of the liquid in the pan. Gradually add the cream, stirring from time to time to keep it from curdling. If the gravy is too thick, thin it with a little milk. Add the parsley and adjust the seasonings. Serve as gravy over the cracker hash, or over boiled potatoes.

SOURCE: Deborah H. Parker and Jane E. Weeden. *Indiana W.C.T.U. Hadley Industrial School Cook Book.* (Indianapolis: Organizer Print, 1884), 25.

HOPPIN JOHN

1907

This is similar to a recipe I learned as a child from Bertha Cole, my grandmother's longtime friend, maid, and household general. Bertha was from South Carolina, knew all about "hoodoo" and the evil eye, and taught me how to cuss. Regarding the ingredients for hoppin john, she preferred ham broth to water. She added a pod of cayenne instead of black pepper, and at the very end, some gumbo filé. I remember there were fried breadcrumbs on top when it came to the table and that she always made this for Christmas.

YIELD: 4 TO 6 SERVINGS.

½ cup cowpeas
½ cup diced salt pork
1 large onion (8 ounces), sliced
2 tablespoons molasses
1 quart hot water or ham broth

2 to 3 cups cooked brown rice, or 1 cup uncooked brown rice (see note)
Gumbo filé (see note)
Salt and pepper
Breadcrumbs (optional)

Hoppin John prepared in an eighteenth-century iron "hominy pot."

Cover the cowpeas with boiling water and let stand overnight. In the morning, drain off the excess water and use it when cooking the rice.

Fry the salt pork in a deep pot or kettle. When it begins to get crispy, add the onion and fry until it is very soft and beginning to scorch. Add the peas and molasses and fry a few minutes, then add the water (and cayenne pepper if you choose to do it Bertha's way). Cover and cook until the peas are soft (about 1½ hours). Add the brown rice freshly cooked, enough to absorb most of the liquid. Add the gumbo filé, adjust seasoning, and serve.

NOTE:

Instead of adding cooked rice, one can add uncooked rice about 1 hour after the peas have begun to boil. In this case, it will be necessary to add more water or broth. For the above quantity, ½ teaspoon gumbo filé will thicken the batch; 1 teaspoon will make it very thick, which is how Bertha liked it.

For those unfamiliar with gumbo filé, it is a powder made from ground sassafras leaves. It acts as a thickening agent in soups and gumbos. Gumbo filé is now sold commercially in small jars and is available in the spice sections of most supermarkets.

SOURCE: *Gold Medal Rice Cook Book.* (New Orleans, La.: National Rice Milling Co., 1907), 44.

HAM AND PARSNIPS

Before 1822

This tasty old New Jersey recipe from the Burlington area came to me via the Harmer family of the Wyanoke Dairies in Moorestown. Not just any ham was used. It had to be Newbold ham, for which Burlington was justly famous, even in the eighteenth century. A recipe for "doing up" hams in "the Burlington Manner" appeared in *Kite's Town and Country Almanac for 1822*.[31] But the real Newbold recipe did not come to light until after the death of its jealous owner, William Newbold. It was found hidden in his cellar wall and subsequently published in the *Burlington Gazette*. YIELD: 4 SERVINGS.

5 medium parsnips (about 1¼ pounds), peeled and cut into 2 x ½-inch pieces
½ cup water
6½ ounces country-style ham, diced
4 tablespoons unsalted butter
1 tablespoon all-purpose flour

½ cup milk
1 tablespoon sugar
2 teaspoons Dijon mustard
¼ teaspoon salt
2 tablespoons white vinegar
1 tablespoon chopped parsley

Put the parsnips and water in a saucepan and bring to a boil. Reduce the heat to low and simmer, covered, for 5 minutes. Add the ham and simmer until the parsnips are tender (about 10 minutes).

While the parsnips are cooking, melt the butter in a small saucepan over low heat. Stir in the flour with a whisk and cook for 1 minute, stirring constantly. Add the milk, sugar, mustard, and salt. Stir in the vinegar and bring to a simmer.

Drain the parsnips and ham and transfer to a serving dish. Top with the mustard gravy and garnish with the parsley.

SOURCE: Marion W. Harmer. Handwritten Recipe. (Moorestown, New Jersey, 1914). Roughwood Collection.

OPPOSITE PAGE: **Ham and parsnips with mustard dressing, an early New Jersey folk dish.**

Redware bake pot with glazed
interior. Pennsylvania, circa 1815–1825.
(Philadelphia Museum of Art)

GUMBIS

1842

YIELD: 6 TO 8 SERVINGS.

1 meaty, well-flavored ham hock
1 quart water
4 large, tart apples pared, cored, and sliced (Winesap apples are recommended)
½ head cabbage, coarsely shredded

4 medium onions, sliced
1 cup slab bacon, cubed
2 six-inch veal sausages, sliced (optional)
Salt and pepper

Simmer the ham hock in the water for at least 2 hours, or until the meat is falling from the bone and the broth is reduced to 2 or 3 cups. Strain the broth and reserve. Pick the meat from the bone and break it up into small pieces. Discard the bone and any excess fat.

Preheat the oven to 350°F.

In a 4- or 5-quart enameled pot, or glazed earthenware container similar to the one pictured, make layers of the ingredients in the following order: a layer of sliced apple, then cabbage, onion, bacon, sausage, and meat from the ham hock. Cover this with another layer each of apple, cabbage, onion, and meat, and repeat until all of the ingredients are used up. The top layer should always consist of cabbage, even if it means departing from this order. Season with salt and pepper and add ¾ cup of the broth reserved from the ham hock. Use the remaining broth to moisten the Gumbis if it becomes too dry during baking. Cover the pot with a snug-fitting lid and bake for 1 hour. Check from time to time to be certain it is not too dry. When the Gumbis is done, stir it up with a spoon and serve from the pot.

NOTE:

There are many variations to this basic one-pot dish. Some people prefer it "stewy" and add more broth; others take the unused broth, thicken it with browned flour (roux), and pour it like gravy over the dish. Plainer versions eliminate the sausage, sometimes even the bacon. Too much meat will spoil it; but for the Pennsylvania Dutch, one can never add too many onions or too much cabbage.

SOURCE: George Girardey. *Höchst nützliches Handbuch über Kochkunst.* (Cincinnati, Ohio: J. A. James, 1842), 4.

From *The Useful and the Beautiful* (Philadelphia, 1850).
(Roughwood Collection)

*E*lizabeth Lea's scoring of the johnny cake, the shellaclike glaze on Worcester loaf, curds molded in the form of a heart, wafers pressed with "pretty devices," preserved watermelon "carved with the taste of a sculptor"; we have already encountered references to some of these tantalizing and suggestive ornamental touches. But is there an overarching "folk aesthetic"? Is there a set of principles or an unspoken code that dictates to the folk cook what is art and what is not?

In his essay on ornamental cookery, Roland Barthes discussed the disturbing hold on us that food achieves when it is idealized in photography through artifice, garnish, ornament, and presentation.[1] The camera's eye, which created these vignettes of supposedly edible perfection, becomes the telescoped vision of the viewer. Through it, the viewer is tempted with an impression of an existence that is quite outside firsthand experience. It is an image of food that cannot be touched or tasted, yet it becomes fixed in the mind as though it had in fact existed. Intellectual cookery, the art cookery of chefs and confectioners trained in the manipulation of the senses, relies a great deal on the shifting lenses of this vicarious vision. It is the packaging of image; it is the created illusion of connectedness.

In 1915 a manufacturer of bread in this country announced that he had discovered the source of "homemade flavor," an immense breakthrough considering that most

Left, professional copper aspic mold, circa 1885; *right*, folk aspic mold, circa 1880, soldered together from tin pie pans and cookie cutters.

women at the time still baked their own bread.[2] It has been nearly seventy-five years since that culinary sputnik was launched. We see its fallout everywhere, but I think it is safe to say that at some point along the way, the frightful idea of an elixir of instant connectedness tumbled back to earth and quietly deflated somewhere in the jungle. It reminds me of yet another breakthrough: diet mayonnaise made with mineral oil.[3]

The sensibilities of the folk cook have been battered for a long time by the onslaught of such inventions. Her extraordinary resiliency has drawn strength to a large measure from her ability—like that of the Amish farmwife—to keep the realities of her immediate world separate from such intrusions. Whether or not you or I consider her handiwork "art" is of far less significance to her than how she perceives it in her own eyes. Because, through that unique filter, all things around her are focused on relationships based on family and extended kinships and the many communal attitudes that give her art its context and meaning.

OPPOSITE PAGE: Children toasting bread the old-fashioned way. Wood engraving from *Table Talk*, February 1893.

Toast and Morning Glories: The "Cracker" Aesthetic

While discussing the subject of broiled oysters on toast, Philadelphia restaurateur James Parkinson lamented in 1879: "Take no liberty with it until you have qualified yourself to make the sweet and rich brownish-red and reddish-brown toast, after the manner of the Queen Anne housekeepers of a former generation. I am reminded," he continued, "that since the introduction of ranges, good old-time toast has become well-nigh a lost art."[4]

It is true, we take toast for granted today and none of it is any the better for it. Toast, properly done, was one of the unsung accomplishments of American folk cookery. It was a culinary art form reduced by its very nature to the perfection of classic simplicity. It represented a craftsmanship in folk cookery that has little to do with ornament.

In dealing with toast, we should keep in mind first of all that the bread was most likely homemade. This implied that the bread tasted generally of the grain from which the flour or meal was ground. The grain may have been inexpensive, the flour coarse, but the toast would have been done more or less the same way: with a *toasting fork*. Caroline Gilman remarked in 1859

that toasting irons (as opposed to forks) were a luxury "so little known in some places, where forks are destroyed daily in *burning* one piece of bread, while the iron *toasts* three in less time."[5]

Mrs. Gilman's evident haste did not make the toast brown better. But a slow, patient drying out of each slice until it turned a caramel red improved even middling bread with such surprising results that one could not hope to compare it with the packaged rusks of today, the next best thing.

This very simple article of food, which was usually made on the end of a long wrought-iron fork—the handle might be three feet in length—was one of the most commonly consumed and universally liked of all American quick snacks before the coming of the cookstove. It was considered a healthy way to start the morning; William Byrd of Virginia mentioned that he had toast and cider for breakfast in 1709.[6] But the only way to learn the art of getting the toast right was by watchful imitation side by side with an accomplished cook. The characteristic nutty flavor, the crisp texture, the required color—all of these subtle degrees of perfection could only be experienced at the hearth.

Parkinson was correct. The cookstove produced a different kind of heat that made toasting the old way impossible; and coal

fumes did not improve taste either. In any case, with a cookstove, the challenge was to take up pastry baking; thus, the cook turned her energies to other, sweeter luxuries. And how much better they tasted when the recipe came from a cookbook!

Folk cookery was to some extent dictated by cookbook literature, even when many cooks could not read. People who do not read have amazing abilities to connect with people who do and to commit to memory things that many literate people forget in a moment. Historically, there was a definite perception that cookbook cookery and folk cookery were separate genres, even though they borrowed from one another. The one was middle class (more likely upper middle class), while the other, to use a tidewater expression, was *cracker,* meaning "backwoods."

An article under "Chats in the Kitchen" in *The Household,* a Brattleboro, Vermont, monthly of the 1870s, remarked on the differences between "family" soups and "cookbook" soups.[7] A cookbook soup was "usually made to be eaten merely as 'first course,' and [is] made by straining the broth and having all the meat and fat removed." The other, "a good, healthy family dinner," was composed of broth with the meat left in, along with added vegetables or what "commodiments" were on hand. It is evident from this that progressive cookbook literature was viewed with a certain degree of suspicion by old-style cooks in the 1870s. The cookbook offered ways of doing things that were aimed more at refinement than at the communal network upon which folk cooks relied for raw materials and inspiration.

This resistance was one reason for the development of "folksy" commentators on food in publications intended for a rural readership. The *American Agriculturist* in the 1850s and 1860s featured "Aunt Hattie"; *Der Amerikanische Bauer* (The Amer-

Butter paddle or "spade" of bird's-eye maple, circa 1840, is an example of folk esthetic of line and form determined by function.

ican Farmer), a Pennsylvania Dutch monthly of the 1850s, featured a feisty "Aunt Pall"; the *Rural New Yorker,* published in Rochester, always contained a section on "Domestic Economy"; and *Arthur's Home Magazine,* a reformist, Temperance-oriented weekly in Philadelphia, even went so far as to give away free sewing machines to every woman who brought in thirty-five subscribers—a highly successful readership campaign.

The ulterior goal of all the magazines aimed at conservative, rural cooks was to induce them to buy the products depicted in the copious advertising. Those pictures showing the latest styles in cakes, butter carving, and newfangled pots and pans certainly did plant new images in the minds of many readers—particularly the young.

The Lily or Morning Glory Cake by Norma Schrope, facing the title page of this book, is an example of this insinuation of ideas into rural cookery. This cake is made of sponge-cake "horns" dipped in colored icing and arranged with the pointed ends of the horns facing the middle. The recipe for this cake was widely circulated in church newspapers in the 1870s and 1880s, and as a result, it appeared in quite a few charitable cookbooks of the period. It was the perfect thing for a church dinner or bazaar, a prize in fund-raising raffles, and, as in the case of Norma Schrope's

cake, a culinary tour de force for a large family reunion. The social dimensions of the cake were, in fact, far more important than the ingredients (or the taste), for it served as a substitute *pièce montée,* the sugarwork structure that Victorian upper-class families in town displayed on their banquet tables.

When we speak of food as art form, we often think of these confectionery pieces, of ornamental cakes, or of bread twisted into myriads of shapes, like the showpiece or "trophy" breads of eighteenth- and nineteenth-century American bakers. This form of decorative food was usually the product of professional cookery. The measure by which we judge it is somewhat different from that by which we judge folk cookery, even though, aesthetically, they

Baker's trophy bread, from an 1899 woodcut.

follow the same rules of structure and form. Folk cookery is measured by what it *does*, how it interconnects with its social setting. This is the only criterion used to determine its survival, because in folk cookery, foods that no longer serve a purpose are quickly forgotten.

It goes without saying that there are also many levels of folk cookery, from the extreme poverty cookery of Appalachia, to the homey productions of the minister's wife, who may have learned a number of things about professional cookery in a young lady's seminary. She might even have taught cooking to a circle of young women in her husband's church.

In contrast to "family" cookery, the eighteenth- and nineteenth-century term for folk cookery, cookery that was "not right," not up to standards, was often termed "bachelor," since bachelors were not supposed to know how to cook. Bachelors did cook, of course, and they were the brunt of a vast body of humorous cooking lore. This shows up in eighteenth- and nineteenth-century recipe names like Bachelor's Loaf (also called Federal Cake—a political comment there), Bachelor's Pone, and Bachelor's Bread.[8]

Bachelor's Bread is actually a cake. The pan is lined on the bottom with large, thin slices of citron and split almonds and then filled with sponge-cake batter. After bak-ing, it is turned out fruit-side up. Today, we use sliced canned pineapples instead of citron and call it upside-down cake. The folk cook found humor in this kind of recipe because by being "upside-down," it poked fun at sexual orientation and inversions of accepted social roles.

Many of these folk concepts have not appeared in dictionaries of Americanisms because the compilers are not yet aware of the complex vocabularies of food. Likewise, "folk aesthetic" as a species of design is still largely defined by ornament rather than by function.[9] In folk cookery, necessity determines form. But there are two more or less distinct ways of defining what is considered "beautiful." One uses organic criteria, whereby a utensil, with extraordinary economy of line and ornament, meets the functional requirements of its intended purpose—a butter paddle or rolling pin designed to fit a specific person's hand, for example.

The other is the decorative criterion, whereby the folk artist fills empty surfaces with pictorial or three-dimensional "stories." The carved gingerbread board occupies this category since the picture is mnemonic, an image associated with a popular song, a folk tale, or perhaps a morality story.

Likewise, when a cook makes "bird tracks" in the crust of her green tomato pie

Pie with "bird track" decoration, from an 1887 woodcut.

(to serve as steam vents), she is alluding to oral traditions she heard at the side of a great-aunt or grandmother.[10] Perhaps she no longer knows or remembers that her bird-track patterns resemble sprigs of rosemary, or that in seventeenth-century America, gilded sprigs of rosemary were stuck into roasts and pies on tables of colonial gentry. For her, bird tracks tell stories about the chickadee that feeds near her window, about the day she made the apron she is wearing. Bird tracks remind her of things she likes to remember. Ornament in folk cookery is thus like the Egyptian hier-

oglyph. It is a symbol to aid the memory and please the eye.

The aesthetics of function, whereby form is ordered by need, determined the variety of designs and types of vessels once used to store pickled or preserved foods. The shape of these vessels was directly related to what went into them and so too was the material from which they are made. Ornament was superfluous because it did not contribute to the intended functional purpose. Certainly, if ornament was there, it could never interfere with function.

The genteel cook in colonial America spent a large portion of her time putting up produce for winter use. The supplies she laid in were crucial to the welfare of the house, a fact of which she was most acutely aware. The measure of her ability —her social function as wife and mistress of a large property—was often put to test at table, and so it was that genteel cookbooks promoted showpiece recipes, "French tricks" as cookbook writer Hannah Glasse so aptly called them in 1747.

West India gherkins, mentioned as "best for pickles, but generally bitter" by Amelia Simmons in her 1796 cookbook;[11] pickled radish pods (pods of radish tops allowed to "bolt" or go to seed); pickled barberries— a popular fish garnish; pickled purslane— all of these were used as food ornaments in

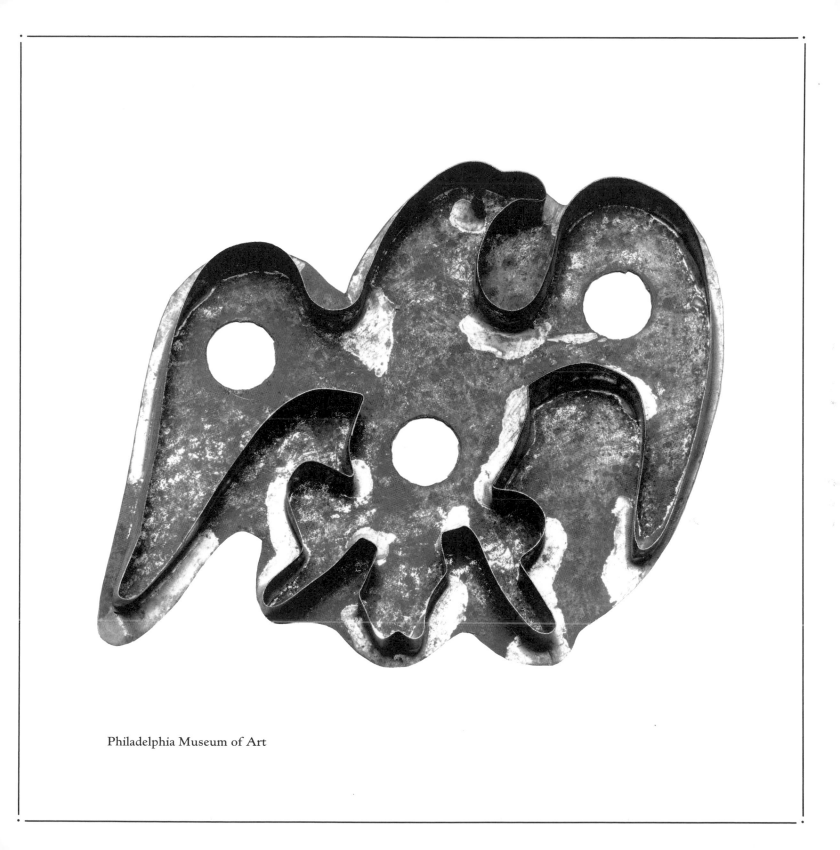

Pickled West India Gherkins
with Bay Leaves

Pickled Purslane
and Lima Beans

Pickled Radish Pods with
Ginger, Allspice, and Mace

Pickled Barberries

upper-class cookery. They were the kind of side-dish fare one would expect to find at Roseland Plantation in South Carolina or at a merchant's house in Philadelphia or Boston.

Even though they may have been made at home—one of the general criteria for folk cookery—these recipes required somewhat unusual ingredients: fresh bay leaves in the case of the gherkins, not to mention the gherkins themselves; white wine in the case of the purslane. And most important, they required glass or special stone pots because these were delicate pickles with low acidity, and that meant that they were difficult to keep. In eighteenth-century America, most rural people could not afford such luxuries or the time required to make them. Effort had to be concentrated on simple things that worked.

Cucumbers were more difficult to grow than the weedy West India gherkins, but they were easier to pickle, and they could be made in large enough quantities to warrant the trouble. Hoofland's almanac for 1875 described the old method of preparing them: "Place them in a stoneware firkin, and cover with good strong cider vinegar, adding a small quantity of whole cloves, allspice, pepper and mustard."[12] Melon and pepper "mangoes" were also put up in stone "firkins." A recipe for them is included at the end of this chapter.

Firkin is rarely, if ever, defined as a "crock" in English and American dictionaries, yet in American kitchen dialect, this is the most common use of the word. There is even a verb, *to firkin,* meaning to pack something into a firkin. The term is of considerable age, coming from Early English *ferdekyn* (*vierde,* meaning "fourth" + *-kyn,* a diminutive ending). It generally meant a fourth of something, as in a fourth part of a barrel. Commercially, firkins were small wooden casks of varying size used for butter and lard. Evidently, in American dialect, the firkin *shape* was enough to qualify a thing as a firkin.

Stoneware firkins, like the wooden ones, were round-bottomed with straight sides. Imagine a tin can, and you will have just imagined a miniaturized firkin. Stoneware firkins in the nineteenth century came in many sizes, some as large as fifty gallons—I still have the twenty-gallon firkin my great-grandfather used for making sauerkraut. Actually, most cooks preferred smaller firkins—three to five gallons—as in the recipe quoted. Otherwise, when filled with pickles, they were too heavy to move.

The stoneware firkin was as basic to folk cookery in the eighteenth and nineteenth centuries as the refrigerator is today. The short broad firkins, about a foot high, often had lids and were used as "cake crocks,"

Stoneware firkin, or cake crock, with lid, circa 1870. Courtesy of the Henry Francis du Pont Winterthur Museum.

that is, places to store and mellow fruitcakes or cakes being cut and used over a period of time.

Stoneware, which was fired at a high temperature and usually salt-glazed, was preferred for food storage and pickling because the clay body was more impervious to moisture than earthenware and because salt glaze did not react chemically with strong food acids like vinegar—a fact well understood in colonial America. For this reason, soured milk, or *clabber,* as it was called, and salted butter were also stored in stoneware vessels.

The shape of the stoneware firkin, with its broad open mouth, allowed for easy ac-

Cooking manual by jar manufacturer Solomon B. Rowley, Lockport, New York, 1870. (Roughwood Collection)

cess to the contents, and in the case of pickled cucumbers or mangoes, where high acidity reduced or hindered the breakdown of enzymes, the pickles remained "safe" as long as they were kept under the brine. This was often accomplished by boiling an old china plate in strongly salted water (to sterilize it), then placing it in the firkin to hold the pickles down. To insure against spoilage, it was best to keep the vegetables at least two inches below the surface of the pickle.

More delicate pickles, such as pickled peaches or eggs, where acidity was not as high, required vessels that were more closed at the top to reduce contact with the air. For that reason, stoneware jars with narrow mouths were preferred. Generally speaking, the term *jar* in American folk cookery meant that the neck of the vessel was restricted in some way. The shape of the earliest commercial fruit jars mimicked the older stoneware forms.

Country potters in the nineteenth century depended for a large part of their income on the production of jars and firkins, a product of the important "networking" they once had with country cooks. When commercial glass houses began to mass-market the canning jar in the 1850s and 1860s, many potteries tried to respond with local innovations. John Bell of Waynesboro, Pennsylvania, made yellowware fruit jars in the 1850s that were similar to those made in factories. H. H. Melick of Roseville, Ohio, made stoneware jars that imitated patented glass ones. And in the 1880s a number of Illinois potteries produced the brown "Peoria" tomato jars that have an almost oriental quality of design and finish. In Maine, many potteries adapted the fruit-jar form for pickling oysters or for shipping them fresh to market.[13]

All of these localized fruit-jar adaptations used patented tin lids that were held in place with a cement made from rosin, brick dust, and beeswax.[14] The necks of the stoneware bottles used for catsups were also dipped in this compound. It was necessary to chip the hardened cement with a sharp instrument in order to get at the tin lid and lift it. The oyster knives shown in chapter 1 came in very handy for this purpose. In any case, few of these old jars have survived with mouths intact. They were usually severely damaged by the jabs and blows of frustrated cooks.

Small stoneware jars were often used directly in the cooking process. In her 1881 Illinois cookbook, Mrs. Frances Owens published a recipe for plum or yellow "egg" tomato preserves: "Put sugar and tomatoes in layers in a stone crock. Set it in a moderately heated oven, and cook for 3 hours. When cold, add 2 sliced lemons to each gallon."[15]

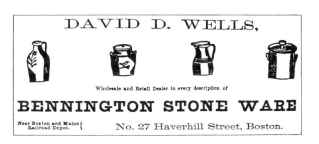

From the Boston city directory for 1859

Ohio preserve jar (with yellow tomatoes) and an 1830s preserve pot tied down with parchment.

German Pickled Tomatoes.
See recipe on page 54.

Preserved Citron Melon
with Lemon, Cardamom,
and Dried Peaches.
See recipe on page 66.

Dilled Green Tomatoes
with Fennel Seed, Ginger,
and Garlic

Small jars, like the Peoria stoneware, could be used to make "German Pickled Tomatoes," one of the recipes at the end of this chapter. This pickle is brown in color because the visual or decorative aspect was still considered by cooks in the 1870s to be less important than the keeping quality. Furthermore, brown sugar was much cheaper than white.

Once glass jars came into general use, the visual ornamentation of pickles grew in importance, since the pickle could be seen through the glass. White sugar gradually replaced brown, because it did not discolor the brine. Neater, more uniformly chopped, sliced, or shredded textures and accents, such as the mixing of red and green peppers—where only green peppers had been used in the past—were introduced to give mixed pickles greater visual interest. The recipe for Higdom in chapter 6 is an example of this reordering of decorative priorities.

On the other hand, the home preservation of meats remained mostly untouched by the canning-jar revolution. To a large measure, this was due to the decline in home butchering after the Civil War and a concurrent growth in the availability of beef. Both were brought about by the commercialization of livestock raising. Thus, American folk cookery underwent a radical reorientation away from salted meats, especially pork, to fresh beef as daily fare.

While the stoneware firkin was sometimes used to store meats, especially when they were collared (pickled in aspic), the more common meat pot was tulip-shaped, smaller at the base than at the top. The least expensive sorts were made of redware, with glazed interiors. The exteriors

Decorative pickles in a "Gem" preserve jar. Original lid and jar, circa 1870.

OPPOSITE PAGE: *(left to right)* Preserve pot (Ohio, circa 1830); "Peoria" tomato jar (Illinois, circa 1865–1875); yellowware fruit jar (Pennsylvania, circa 1855–1860); H. H. Melick stoneware pickle jar (Ohio, circa 1876); and stoneware bottle for catsup (Pennsylvania, circa 1835).

were unglazed and therefore not subject to the kind of whimsical ornamentation often found on stoneware. The rough, unfinished surface of the redware meat pots was not without functional purpose, however: The unfinished surface made them easier to handle and less likely to slip away from wet or greasy hands.

In general, winter sausage was the primary meat put down in crocks, but fried pork ribs and chops were also stored in this manner. Next to them, mincemeat was probably the most popular, since it could serve both as a pie filling and as a breakfast "pudding."

The following recipe is excerpted from a letter sent by a reader of *The Household* magazine in 1874. It describes the common method for making and storing sausage:

> Make the whole batch out in cakes as wanted for table use and fry it till done. Keep a crock standing on the stove and fill in as you fry till nearly full, pouring in the gravy. I then carry it to the cellar, turn a plate over till morning, then take off the weight and finish covering it with hot lard. If the crock is well glazed it will keep good till harvest if kept in a cool place.[16]

The writer was referring, incidentally, to sausage that was put down the previous fall. In other words, sausage could be kept for about a year in this manner.

From Pigweed to Toll House Cookies

On the organic or structural level, creative substitution of ingredients or innovative techniques have often carried folk cookery in new directions. This unceasing reinvention of the old has been a hallmark of folk cookery's extraordinary fertility.

The recipe for preserved citron at the end of this chapter derives its unique flavor from the citron melon, even though the melon is itself a substitute for the subtropical citron (a small evergreen tree) for which recipes like this were devised.

Likewise, the recipe for brandied cherries, by using spices and aniseed, creates a flavor that is intended to approximate the costly Dalmatian liqueur *Maraschino di Zara,* now known as *Maraska Zadar* in Yugoslavia. In the seventeenth and eighteenth centuries, the Venetians traded Maraschino with England and the American colonies, where it was used extensively by the well-to-do in drinks and ices called ratafias. American cherry bounce (also a liqueur) is the folk version of the ratafia. The unctuous, dark, cherry-rich juice from the brandied cherries can be filtered off like cherry bounce and used as a pleasant and rather peacefully potent beverage.

Purslane pie, a folk dish still made in some parts of the Middle States, draws upon the Elizabethan cookery of England for its model. In *The English House-Wife* (1675), Gervase Markham includes a recipe for "Spinach Tart," spinach being much approved of in old English cookery.[17]

Markham's recipe required that the spinach be minced as fine as possible—this difficult-to-achieve texture was a mark of elegance in the days before the food processor. The "pap" was then cooked thick in wine, mixed with white sugar and cinnamon, and reduced to a marmalade that was then thinned slightly with rose water. The hot, flowery preserve was poured into rectangular prebaked tart shells called *coffins* to cool. Once jelled, each tart was garnished with caraway comfits (caraway seeds coated with sugar). The white comfits, laid out in fancy arabesques against the dark green filling, created a delightful lacy effect for the eye and gave a surprising texture to the pie when eaten.

In response to a request for heirloom recipes in a January 1949 Allentown newspaper, a reader from Hereford, Berks County, Pennsylvania, submitted a very old recipe for purslane pie.[18] Purslane, a colonial garden vegetable, is now largely ignored as a pest and referred to unaffectionately as "pigweed." It has a lemony flavor far more intense than that of spinach.

In the purslane pie recipe, the purslane leaves are stripped from the stems, minced fine, and cooked to a pulp with brown sugar and grated lemon zest. As in Markham's recipe, the filling is spiced with cinnamon. Some flour is added to thicken it; then it is baked between two crusts like a fruit pie. It is not exactly Markham's spinach tart, but it is certainly a folk approximation of something very close to it. The top crust, of course, can be ornamented so that it supplies a decorative equivalent of the comfit arabesques.

This kind of creative reinvention is one of the classic traits of folk cookery. Green tomato pie, which is an adaptation of gooseberry pie (using unripe gooseberries); hard-times fruit cake, which blends soft gingerbread with dried apples; and the honey tea cake mentioned all make use of this process of creative adaptation.

In more recent times, we have seen the same forces at work. In 1902, for example, the Honey Comb Chocolate Company of Battle Creek, Michigan, announced its latest edible novelty, the "Honey Comb chocolate chip."[19] Their chips resembled in shape the computer chips of our era, and like computer chips, they were not generally a retail product. Commercial bakeries put the Honey Comb chips in their drop cookies. But for the average home cook, the nearest substitute was small chocolate kisses, a Valentine's confection that is now standard in Toll House cookies.

PICKLED EGGS
1868

During warm weather, when eggs were plentiful, it was customary to put up a large jar of pickled ones to have them on hand during the cold months, when hens stopped laying. Those were the days before heated chicken houses. And in those days pickled eggs were not a substitute for fresh eggs; they were a table relish eaten with other foods, chopped into winter salads, or sliced up in decorative shapes as garnishing on platters of cold meat.

YIELD: 1 DOZEN PICKLED EGGS.

12 hard-boiled eggs, shelled
3 tablespoons sliced gingerroot
1 tablespoon whole peppercorns
1 tablespoon whole allspice
1 teaspoon whole cloves
2 cups vinegar
½ cup sugar
1 teaspoon pickling salt

Put the eggs in a sterilized wide-mouth quart jar, scattering the ginger and spices around them. Scald the vinegar, sugar, and salt for 5 minutes, then pour this over the eggs. Seal and cool. Set in the refrigerator for 1 to 2 weeks before using.

NOTE:

If the eggs are large, use a 2-quart jar and turn it from time to time so that all the eggs are pickled evenly.

SOURCE: *The Agricultural Almanac for 1869.* (Lancaster, Pa.: Printed by John Baer & Son, 1868).

OPPOSITE PAGE: *(left to right)* Four-gallon redware storage crock (Pennsylvania, circa 1820); two-gallon stoneware pickle jar (Baltimore, circa 1815); half-gallon stoneware firkin (Pennsylvania, circa 1885); two-gallon stoneware storage crock (Pennsylvania, circa 1880).

Winter Sausage.
See recipe on page 60.

Pickled Eggs

Pepper and
Melon Mangoes

German Pickled Tomatoes

1870

These sweet-and-sour tomatoes, either whole or pureed, make an extraordinary condiment on meats, especially smoked pork chops. I have added a Pennsylvania Dutch recipe for the latter to demonstrate how it is done.

YIELD: APPROXIMATELY 8 TO 12 PINTS, DEPENDING ON THE SIZE OF TOMATOES USED.

7 pounds plum tomatoes,
the smaller the better
1 tablespoon shredded mace

1 tablespoon whole cloves
3 pounds brown sugar
3 cups red-wine vinegar

Put the tomatoes in a colander and pour scalding water over them to blister the skins. Peel the tomatoes, leaving them whole, and set them in layers in a deep preserving kettle. Scatter the spices between the layers as you work.

Dissolve the sugar in the vinegar and bring to a boil. Boil hard for 5 minutes and take off the scum. Pour over the tomatoes. Cover and let stand 24 hours.

The next day, bring the tomatoes to a boil, taking care to shift them around so that they heat evenly; otherwise, the ones on the bottom will cook too much. The tomatoes will shrivel and resemble figs; this appearance should be maintained throughout the pickling process.

After the tomatoes are hot, boil gently for 5 minutes, or until the fruit is thoroughly heated. Pack the tomatoes in sterilized jars and continue to boil the liquid for about 10 minutes. Pour it over the fruit and seal. Give the jars a 10-minute water bath.

NOTE:

The tomatoes will lose some of their water during the pickling process. As a result, there may be as much as 2 quarts of liquid left over. Do not waste it. Use it to make another western Maryland specialty: sweet-and-sour apple butter. To each 2 quarts of pickling liquid, add 10 apples, pared, cored, and chopped. Cook gently for 4 to 6 hours, stirring from time to time, until thick and smooth. This will yield 2 to 3 pints of apple butter.

SOURCE: *The Queen of the Kitchen.* (Baltimore: Lucas Brothers, 1870), 197.

Broiled Smoked Pork Chops with German Pickled Tomatoes. See recipe on page 56.

YIELD: 4 SERVINGS.

3 tablespoons lightly salted butter
4 smoked pork chops

⅓ cup pickling liquid
⅔ cup chopped pickled tomatoes

Heat the butter in a heavy skillet until it begins to foam. Fry the chops until brown, then remove them from the pan and set aside. Add the pickling liquid to the pan and boil 5 minutes, or until it darkens.

Put the chops in a shallow baking dish and cover with the tomatoes. Pour the hot liquid over this and set under a broiler for 5 minutes, or until the tomatoes begin to caramelize around the edges. Serve immediately.

SOURCE: Interview. Reuben Harnish, April 9, 1972. Lancaster County, Pennsylvania.

DR. ESENWEIN'S TOMATO CATSUP
1912

This was doubtless one of the most popular of all Pennsylvania Dutch catsup recipes and one that captured the spicy, West Indian character of the old-style catsups that came into fashion in American cookery in the 1820s. I should add that Dr. Esenwein was not a cook. He was a well-known druggist and pharmacist in Reading, Pennsylvania, and the manufacturer of several patent medicines. Among these were Dr. Esenwein's Pectoral and Aromatic Balsam, and Kura-Derma, "the great scalp and skin remedy." Furthermore, in all fairness to history, the doctor's recipe probably came from his wife, Kate Daniels, whom he married in 1864. YIELD: 1 QUART.

2¼ cups vinegar
3 tablespoons whole cloves
3 tablespoons whole allspice
1 peck ripe, plum-type tomatoes
¾ cup pickling salt

6 two-inch pods cayenne pepper
1⅔ tablespoons white pepper
1½ heads garlic (3 ounces total),
peeled and beaten to a paste
1 cup sugar

The night before you plan to make the catsup, bring the vinegar to a hard boil for 5 minutes and pour over the cloves and allspice. Cover and infuse until morning. Then strain off the vinegar and measure out 2 cups.

Mash the tomatoes and cook until soft. Then work them through a sieve to strain out the seeds and skins. This should yield approximately 5 quarts of liquid. In any event, you *must* begin with this quantity of cooked tomato. If you are short, cook some more and add them to the batch.

Mix the cooked, strained tomatoes with the 2 cups of infused vinegar. Add the salt, cayenne, white pepper, garlic, and sugar. Cook slowly in a preserving kettle, stirring often, until reduced to 1 quart. Strain out the cayenne pods and put the catsup up in sterilized bottles or small jars. Seal with a 10-minute water bath.

NOTE:
My great-grandmother Weaver made this spicy catsup, and right before bottling it up, she would add, for this proportion, 2 tablespoons of sage-flavored vinegar.

SOURCE: *The Lancaster, (Pa.) General Hospital "Benefit" Cook Book.* (Lancaster, Pa.: Conn & Slote, 1912), 125.

GREEN TOMATO PIE

1839

YIELD: 6 TO 8 SERVINGS.

Short pastry for 2 crusts
1½ pounds green tomatoes
1½ cups dark brown sugar

Juice of 1 lemon
Grated zest of 1 lemon
2 teaspoons powdered ginger

Preheat oven to 350°F.

Line an 8-inch pie dish with pastry.

Pour scalding water over the tomatoes. Remove and discard the skins. Slice the tomatoes as thin as possible, and mix them with the sugar, lemon juice, zest, and ginger. Fill the pie shell and cover with a top crust. Crimp the edges closed and ornament the top with slits and pastry figures. Brush the crust with cold water and sprinkle granulated sugar over it. Bake for approximately 1 hour.

NOTE:

In August 1987, I received a letter regarding traditional green tomato pies from Geraldine Killoran of Marysville, Washington. Her mother was a Quaker born in Westfield, Indiana, and a member of Duck Creek Friends Meeting. She wrote: "My mother simply sliced tomatoes into the lower pie crust and sugared, floured, and spiced them, much as she made apple pie. To her, the tomatoes were best for this use when slightly tinged with cream or pink color." This procedure conforms to the original 1839 recipe.

SOURCE: *The American Housewife.* (New York: Collins, Keese & Co., 1839), recipe # 245.

OPPOSITE PAGE: Green Tomato Pie baked in an old-style shallow pie dish.

Winter Sausage

1845

One of the advantages of homemade sausage is that it can be a lot less expensive than commercial sausage; what is more, one knows exactly what is in it. This recipe has been reduced from 100 pounds of meat to an amount easily prepared in today's kitchen. The predominating flavor is sage, and the high spicing with pepper is normal for recipes from the early nineteenth century. The "taste" is very much a New England one, not surprising since this is essentially a New England fresh sausage—called "fresh" because it is not smoked.

This kind of sausage was only made during the winter months.

In the South, black pepper was often replaced in fresh sausage with cayenne. In the Middle States, thyme or summer savory was usually mixed with sage in the proportion of 2 tablespoons of thyme to every 4 of sage. In this recipe, then, the sage would be reduced to 5 teaspoons, and 2½ teaspoons of powdered thyme or savory would be added.

YIELD: 24 PATTIES OR 12 SERVINGS.

1½ pounds lean pork
1½ pounds fatty pork
1 tablespoon pickling salt

2½ tablespoons powdered sage
1½ tablespoons fresh-ground pepper

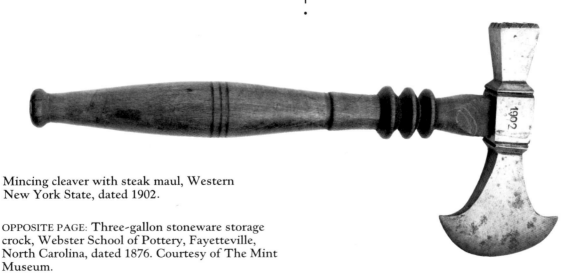

Mincing cleaver with steak maul, Western New York State, dated 1902.

OPPOSITE PAGE: Three-gallon stoneware storage crock, Webster School of Pottery, Fayetteville, North Carolina, dated 1876. Courtesy of The Mint Museum.

Grind the lean and fatty pork together twice. (Your butcher can do this for you; a heavy-duty food processor will also do the job.) Put the meat in a large mixing bowl. Wash your hands thoroughly, or better yet, wear latex gloves. Add the salt, sage, and pepper and work with your hands until all of the seasonings are evenly mixed. If you have a meat grinder or food processor, the seasonings can be added during the second grinding. Form the meat into balls about the size of an egg, then flatten into patties. Wrap individually in cellophane. Pack in freezer bags and freeze until needed.

To fry the sausage, let it thaw, then roll it in flour or fine cracker crumbs. Fry in a heavy skillet until brown on both sides. Allow 2 patties per person.

SOURCE: Josiah T. Marshall. *The Farmer's and Emigrant's Hand-Book.* (New York: D. Appleton & Co., 1845), 165.

BRANDIED CHERRIES

1855

YIELD: 2 QUARTS.

1½ pounds sweet cherries with stems
1½ pounds sugar
1½ cups spring water
Approximately 1 cup
high-proof brandy

4 teaspoons whole cloves
1½ tablespoons whole coriander seed
2 tablespoons aniseed

Stick each cherry with a clean needle and put in a sterilized 2-quart glass jar. Bring the sugar and water to a boil, and boil hard for 5 minutes. Pour this over the cherries, cover, and let stand overnight.

The next day drain off the syrup and boil it again for 5 minutes. Measure out 1½ pints. For each 1½ pints of syrup, use one cup of brandy and the clove, coriander, and aniseed in the amounts listed above.

Clean the jar and sterilize it. Sew the spices into a muslin bag and put the bag in the jar. Cover with the cherries. Mix the syrup and brandy and pour over the fruit. Seal and store in a cool place away from direct sunlight for 1 month. Then remove the bag of spices.

NOTE:

If there is room at the top of the jar after removing the spice bag, I would suggest adding ¼ cup of brandy. The high alcoholic content of the syrup keeps the fruit from spoiling without refrigeration or normal canning procedures.

SOURCE: *Cookery As It Should Be*. (Philadelphia: Willis P. Hazard, 1855), 273.

Fruit jug filled with Brandied Cherries, from Ottawa, Illinois, circa 1887.

Pepper and Melon Mangoes

1914

In seventeenth-century England, stuffed tropical mangoes were imported from India, where this recipe originated. In an effort to reproduce the pickle, English cooks took to "mangoing" all sorts of substitutes, from cucumbers to unripe peaches. Americans, however, preferred baby musk-melons, or, in areas where they did not grow well, bell peppers. Properly made, mango pickles would keep not only all winter but well into the spring. They were served on festive occasions as condiments or decorative garnishes with large roasts of meat. YIELD: 3 QUARTS.

20 small bell peppers, green or
mixed colors
3 quarts water
7½ tablespoons pickling salt
½ pound cabbage, shredded fine
¼ pound fresh-grated horseradish
¼ cup fresh-grated gingerroot
8 teaspoons mustard seed
1 tablespoon powdered mace
1 tablespoon powdered cloves
1 tablespoon powdered cinnamon
½ cup chopped peppers,
mixed colors
20 garlic cloves

PICKLING BRINE:

1½ quarts white vinegar
2½ cups sugar
1 tablespoon pickling salt

Wash the peppers and slit them down the sides. Remove the seeds and veins, and trim the stems, leaving the bases intact. Make a brine of the water and pickling salt and lay the peppers in this overnight. The next day, drain the peppers and discard the brine.

Mix the shredded cabbage, horseradish, gingerroot, mustard seed, spices, and chopped peppers. Put a clove of garlic in each pepper and stuff peppers with the paste. Use clean toothpicks to hold the peppers shut.

Put the peppers in hot, sterilized, wide-mouth jars (three 1-quart jars will be necessary for this recipe). While packing the jars, bring the pickling brine to a boil and boil 5 minutes. Then pour it over the vegetables. Seal the jars and give them a 15-minute water bath.

NOTE:

The stuffing mixture is also sufficient for 20 small melons (total weight about 3 pounds), but the pickling brine must be doubled, and 6 or 7 quart jars will be needed—melons do not pack as tightly as peppers. Otherwise, follow the same procedure as for peppers.

SOURCE: Kate B. Vaughn. *Culinary Echoes from Dixie.* (Cincinnati, Oh.: The McDonald Press, 1914), 251.

PRESERVED CITRON

*T*here are many early American recipes for preserving "citron," and invariably it is citron melon that is intended. Citron melons look like small watermelons, but they have pale green flesh and deep red seeds. They are rampant growers, even in poor soil, prolific fruiters, and are generally free of insects and disease, all of which contributed to their once universal popularity with early American cooks.

Pickled or candied watermelon rind is just one of the many ways citron melon was originally prepared, from preserves in

syrup, to pickles, dry confections, even sliced like apples in pie. This recipe makes a "wet sweetmeat," a rich, sticky dessert food that was especially valued for its visual appeal.

Everything depends on choice of melons and preparation—the older the melons, the more cooking time is needed to tenderize them. In this recipe, however, watermelon rind may be used as a substitute, provided it is not overcooked. An unripe watermelon would be ideal. I must also add that since the original recipe is both vague on certain points of procedure and wastes sugar, I have adjusted it according to the method used by my great-grandmother Essie Hickman, whose manuscript recipe book is now in my possession.

Essie also included a few more things not found in most old citron melon recipes. For example, to each 3-pound batch, she would add 2 tablespoons of whole cardamom seeds and ½ cup of chopped dried peaches. These were stirred into the preserve after it had been boiling hard for 10 minutes. And for decoration, she would put 10 pea-size red crab apples into each pint jar before adding the hot syrup. Crab apples were available because she generally put up her citrons in October, after the other things in the garden were gone. In fact, the mellons could be stored like pumpkins in a dry pantry and preserved during the winter after all the other preserving was out of the way.

YIELD: APPROXIMATELY 8 PINTS OF PRESERVED MELON.

*½ cup fresh gingerroot,
pared and sliced
6 cups spring water or bottled water
5 pounds sugar
3 lemons, seeded and shredded
as for marmalade*

*6 pounds citron melon, pared,
seeded, and cut into cubes (or an
equivalent quantity of watermelon
rind)*

*P*oach the gingerroot in the spring water for 25 minutes, then strain the "tea" and reserve 3½ cups. Save the ginger for later use in the recipe.

Put 1¾ cups hot "tea" in a preserving pan and dissolve 2½ pounds of the sugar in it over medium heat. Add 1½ shredded lemons and boil hard. As soon as the syrup begins to foam, add 3 pounds of the citron (or watermelon) and boil hard for 20 to 25 minutes, or until the fruit begins to look transparent around the edges. Then strain out the fruit and pack in sterile jars. Reduce the syrup to the consistency of honey, pour over the fruit, and seal.

Repeat as above with the remaining 3 pounds of citron or watermelon. If there is syrup left over, do not waste it. Pour it over the reserved ginger and boil the ginger until the syrup reaches the soft ball stage. Remove the ginger and spread it on wire racks to drain. If the humidity is low, the ginger will dry in 2 or 3 days. If it is slightly sticky, so much the better. Roll it in coarse sugar and store in an airtight container.

N O T E :

Keep in mind when cubing the melon that it will shrink by as much as 50 percent as it cooks. Always weigh the fruit after paring and seeding it.

SOURCE: *The American Family Keepsake.* (Boston: H. B. Skinner and J. B. Hall, 1848), 51.

From a 1907 postcard
(Roughwood Collection)

*I*f we have a national dish," commented a writer in *Hearth and Home,* "we suppose its name is pie. The line between winter and spring is accurately defined in the minds of half the housewives in the country as the time when there is nothing to make pies of. Dried apples are used up, prunes are too expensive, and rhubarb has not made its appearance."[1]

Since pie is found in every part of the country, it is one consistent source of evidence for regionalization in American folk cookery. Cookbook literature is full of examples of this, from the potato pudding pies of Maryland; the ground cherry pies of Pennsylvania; and the white whortleberry pies of Kent County, Delaware; to the boiled cider pies of New England; and the vinegar pies of the Upper Midwest. In each of these examples, the process of creative substitution has resulted in an identifiable local or regional trait.

Yet the movement of ideas that created these traits did not necessarily flow outward from the "culture hearths" described by Henry Glassie. In fact, the movement of ideas and the creation of "folk" styles are dependent on several overlapping culture hearths, since ideas move vertically, up or down in society, as well as horizontally across the map. The vinegar pie and boiled cider pie recipes at the end of this chapter are but two examples of culinary regionalisms.

The vinegar pie recipe that I have selected is not exactly the same as the vinegar pie now associated so closely with folk festivals in Oklahoma or Iowa. The recipe was published in Detroit, and that is about as close to the source of invention as we may come. It is an adaptation, through substitution, of the baked lemon pudding introduced to American cookery by the confectioner Elizabeth Goodfellow (1767–1851) of Philadelphia and much commented upon by her protégée Eliza Leslie.[2]

Mrs. Goodfellow's pudding, now known as lemon meringue pie, was at one time a mark of great luxury in the high cookery of Philadelphia and New York, requiring as it did many fresh eggs, sweet-cream butter, and fresh lemons—and thus considerable expense. The vinegar pie recipe reduces the lemons to a mere hint of grated zest and replaces them with vinegar. The result looks like lemon meringue pie, but the taste is not the same. This species of vinegar pie became a feature of hotel and boarding-house cookery in the Upper Midwest, doubtless because this part of the country was far enough away from coastal ports to make the cost of lemons prohibitive.

The Browns, in *America Cooks,* put the recipe in their chapter on North Dakota and called it "Pioneer Vinegar Pie."[3] I would rather they had put it in Michigan. This "pioneer" recipe was further altered by midwestern cooks to a species of vinegar pie consisting of sugar, one egg, flour, and a spoonful of sharp vinegar. It was baked between two crusts like the purslane pie mentioned in chapter 2. This is truly a folk technique; the use of two crusts makes this pie a close relative of the pasty, a portable pie that is baked between crusts made of bread dough. Pasties were very popular in early America because they could be eaten in the field or while traveling. They were a snack food consumed when one was away from home and could not make toast.

The shallow, bowled redware "pie" dishes of the eastern part of the United States were used for making pasty pies, which is why these dishes eventually acquired the name of *pie plates.* Technically speaking, pie dishes should be flat-bottomed, round, or rectangular, and generally smaller at the bottom than at the top; in short, a version of the *coffin* mentioned by Gervase Markham in chapter 2.

The shallow pie dish just described was used in Elizabethan and English baroque cookery for baked puddings. The dish was lined with short crust and filled with a rich custard, as in the case of American pumpkin "pie." Anywhere else in the English-speaking world, our pumpkin pie would be called a pudding.

What we have just outlined is a filter-down process from high cookery to folk, from Mrs. Goodfellow and her famous pastry shop in Philadelphia to the sod houses of Kansas and Oklahoma. Overlaying Glassie's map of the rural culture hearths in which folk cookery developed are other culture hearths, so-called elite or urban culture hearths, which also sent out waves of new ideas into the hinterlands and down or up through the various levels of society. Philadelphia, like Newport, Rhode Island, was a major culture hearth in the eighteenth century, so much so that it evolved a distinctive cookery of its own quite apart from that of the outlying counties. One of Philadelphia's folk foods was pepperpot. Another was scrapple. And in the 1880s it gave us peanut butter and the hoagie sandwich.[4] In the 1980s, New York and Los Angeles serve as two important urban culture hearths.

Mrs. Goodfellow almost single-handedly created a "Philadelphia style" through the influence of her cooking school and through Eliza Leslie, who churned out hundreds of Goodfellow recipes in her long career as a cookbook writer. On the folk level, there were individuals in each community who served as focal points for creative cookery. As with folk artists, talent was concentrated in a few hands, and these individuals in turn often served as filters through which ideas entered or left the community. Usually, their culinary talents were well known locally, and other cooks would turn to them for advice, recipes, and training.

Quite often, if a woman was widowed and left without any means of self-support, she would turn her energies to keeping a

Pennsylvania pie crimper made from a George I coin, dated 1753. (Philadelphia Museum of Art)

boardinghouse (as in the case of Eliza Leslie's mother) or open a cake-and-mead shop. From this shop in the front room of her house she sold cakes, cookies, and small beers—sweet, nonalcoholic beverages. As one might imagine, cake-and-mead shops became the favored haunts of children and teenagers.

The Role of Cookbooks in Regionalization

In analyzing regional styles of cookery, we often look at regional cookbooks for clues, but this can be somewhat deceiving when it comes to folk cookery. Mary Randolph's *Virginia Housewife,* Lettice Bryan's *Kentucky Housewife,* Sarah Rutledge's *Carolina Housewife,* Mrs. Howland's *New England Housekeeper,* and Mrs. Benjamin Chew Howard's *Fifty Years in a Maryland Kitchen*—all of these cookbooks are generally treated as though they represent the cookery of the state mentioned in their titles. In part they do, as they all contain some local recipes—Sarah Rutledge's directions for graveling rice, for example, are particularly interesting. But these authors were all women of means—well-educated members of upper-class society—and they had their own social prejudices about folk culture and the working man.

American folk cookery, at least by the nineteenth century, produced its own counterparts to "polite" culinary literature, and in those sourcebooks we find much better evidence of regional folk styles. Among these are *The Family's Guide* (Cortland, N.Y., 1833), *The Approved Recipe Book* (Plainfield, N.J., 1839), Elizabeth Ellicott Lea's *Domestic Cookery* (Baltimore, 1851), Phebe Mendall's *New*

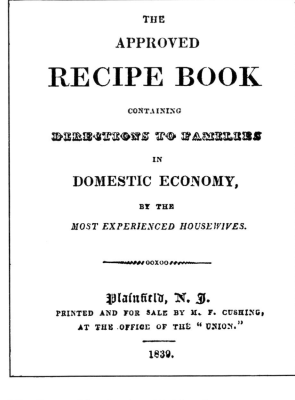

THE

APPROVED

RECIPE BOOK

CONTAINING

DIRECTIONS TO FAMILIES

IN

DOMESTIC ECONOMY,

BY THE

MOST EXPERIENCED HOUSEWIVES.

᛫᛫᛫᛫ OOXOO ᛫᛫᛫᛫

Plainfield, N. J.

PRINTED AND FOR SALE BY M. F. CUSHING,
AT THE OFFICE OF THE "UNION."

1839.

The first cookbook printed in New Jersey.
Courtesy of Mr. Joseph Felcone.

Bedford Practical Receipt Book (New Bedford, Mass., 1859), and one of the best, Frances Owens's *Cook Book and Useful Household Hints* (Chicago, 1881). Both Elizabeth Lea and Phebe Mendall were widows. Lea's husband had been a miller turned orchardist; Mendall's husband had been a whaler. Mrs. Owens, perhaps aware that old ways were dying quickly, included some remarkable material in her book, including a recipe for roasting groundhog.[5]

Even a detailed book like Elizabeth Lea's, which I analyzed and republished in 1982, fails to cover all of the complex nuances of a given regional style.[6] First of all, the use of state boundaries to define regional folk culture creates a highly artificial model. Folk cultures in Europe, for example, have not historically conformed to national boundaries, and governments have spent the past century weeding out pockets of people left on the wrong side of the borders. This same process has taken place in food, with writers of cookbooks, since the nineteenth century, taking the lead in creating the image of ethnically homogenized national cuisines. Such cookbooks are sometimes far more eloquent in their omissions than in their contents.

Henry Glassie's pioneering map suggests only the barest beginnings of larger patterns of regionalization and localization. It would be useful to see how such patterns worked on different levels of folk cookery. Unfortunately, cultural geographers have not yet mapped out the borders of many of these culinary subregions. Thus, Glassie's map, though our only point of reference, remains at best a thumbnail sketch.

Regionalization and Native Foods

Because of the folk cook's connectedness with community and environment, she is most likely to draw on local foodstuffs for ingredients in her cookery. Economic realities will determine her choices. The use of local foods gives character to her dishes, and this in turn becomes a symbol to outsiders of her "style." If she uses an ingredient such as gumbo filé, which is common in Cajun cooking, then she becomes part of this larger regional style. It does not necessarily make her Cajun.

Maple-sugar candy springs to mind as a typically New England confection, and a map could be drawn across the eastern United States showing where the major stands of maple trees are situated. Maple sugar is associated with New England because it is a commercial product there, but the making of maple syrup and sugar for local consumption is far more widespread. Nora Roy, for example, has studied

present-day sugar makers in southern Indiana.[7] The *Kentucky Gazette* for October 31, 1795, mentioned that Benjamin Stout was selling "country made" maple sugar from his store in Lexington.

In the early colonial period, maple sap was used like molasses to make "molasses" beer, fermented to make a sweet wine, and distilled to make a species of whisky called "maple rum." The techniques for doing this were well known in Scotland, where birch sap was used in the same manner.[8]

Another folk beverage, called "spruce beer," was made over a broad area of the eastern United States. It was considered a health drink and was one of the "small beers" popular with cake-and-mead-shop customers. In New England, the tips of black spruce branches, or birch sap, were used to flavor the beer. In the Middle

Cohee *quaich* or drinking vessel from Hampshire County, West Virginia, circa 1780.

States, where black spruce and birch are not commonly found, hemlock branches or sassafras were used instead. In the South, the use of sassafras or sarsaparilla predominated. Thus, in the case of spruce beer, each region had characteristic flavoring ingredients. The same was true of punch.

The punch of colonial taverns and gentlemen's gatherings generally consisted of water, rum or brandy, lemons, sugar, and green tea. The word *punch* comes from the Hindi *panch,* meaning "five"—there are five ingredients.[9] These ingredients, to one degree or another, were all expensive in colonial times, hence the high status of the drink. I might add that the porcelain or silver punch bowls were themselves symbols of considerable social status.

The folk cook devised ways to make punch that would maintain status, while circumventing cost and rarity of ingredients. Wooden punch bowls were used—references to them appear as early as 1732.[10] In the coastal states, lemons were generally replaced with limes, which came into port towns from the Caribbean almost weekly and were many times cheaper than Spanish or Portuguese lemons. Tea was thus the primary expense, since West Indian rum was cheap. In the Middle Atlantic region, wild teaberry leaves were used instead of imported tea; in the coastal South, youpon leaves were the commonest

substitute—"cracker punch" to those who disapproved of such concoctions. Such negative stereotyping is common to all folk cultures, both by members of the group and by outsiders. Much stereotyping is based on food and eating habits—*blazon populaire.*

The word *tuckahoe* (literally, the green arrow arum, of eastern American bogs and swamps) was used as a term for Virginians living east of the Blue Ridge Mountains. On one level, *tuckahoe* implied *lowlanders,* people with their feet in the mud. It was a label of contempt among the "Cohees," the Scotch-Irish mountain folk of central and southwestern Pennsylvania, western Maryland, and western Virginia. Cohee cookery is a regional style of cooking sometimes called "Upper Appalachian"; it has not been studied in great detail.

On another level, *tuckahoe* implied a contempt for Virginia diet, because the tuckahoe was used in colonial and precolonial times as a source of food. Therein lies the rub. Indians harvested the root in late summer and baked it. It has properties similar to manioc, and when exposed to heat, breaks down into starch. This starch was mixed with cornmeal to lighten Indian breads, in much the same way that cooks today mix wheat flour with cornmeal. Poor Virginians who had no wheat flour used tuckahoe instead.

Well-to-do colonial Virginians used the tuckahoe starch to make blancmange, a sweet dessert pudding; to thicken sauces; and to starch their ruffs. The starch worked very much like arrowroot, which happens to be the tuckahoe's botanical first cousin.

What is more, the Cohees were white-potato eaters; the Virginians were sweet-potato eaters. The root of the tuckahoe looks like a sweet potato, and thus, in the eyes of the Cohee, like "Indian food," a thing of ultimate disgust.

Similar, but less polarized, forms of negative stereotyping based on foods have existed in many other parts of the country. In southern Illinois, for example, the basic dietary triad in the early part of this century consisted of potatoes, beans, and pork. According to studies conducted by John Bennett in 1942, people of German heritage in this part of the state consumed more beef than pork and raised more extensive vegetable gardens. Hence, they were also more deeply involved in home canning. A unique article of their diet was blood pudding (*Blutwurst*), which other groups in the area disdained. Fishermen, who drew their livelihood from the Ohio River, consumed the least meat and sold most of their catch in exchange for "farm food"—their term for any kind of produce. The tenant farmers, even when they owned cattle and chickens, generally sold their produce in order to make ends meet. Blacks living in the area were generally landless and were only casual gardeners. They depended for their food on local stores or wild plants such as grapes, poke, elderberry, wild mustard, dandelion, broom sage, and dock. The eating of muskrat was a local stereotype for their diet, just as blood sausage was a stereotype for the Germans.[11]

Farming Patterns and
Regional Styles:
The Meaning of Bread

The agricultural patterns that evolved in this country shaped the various regional styles of folk cookery. In the eighteenth century, the large dairy economy that was centered in Connecticut—an area that had been known for its cheese—moved westward across New York State with the opening of new farmland. By the late 1820s, this shift continued into Ohio, where cheap land and proximity to Great Lakes shipping gave Ohio dairymen an edge over their New England competition. Milk not only became the most common table beverage in Ohio, it also figured in the development of local white-gravy cookeries.[12] Today, this dairy culture has shifted even further west and is now centered in Wisconsin, where climate and land use favor large-scale dairy operations.

The wheat basket of colonial America was situated in northern Maryland and southeastern Pennsylvania before the 1780s, and like the Connecticut "cheese basket," it too moved westward with the migration of farmers in search of better wheat-growing soils. For a brief time, the wheat belt paused in western New York State, in the Genesee Valley, then moved into Ohio and later into Illinois and the Upper Great Plains, where wheat could be grown more economically on a large scale.[13] As the center of wheat growing moved west, it left in its trail a large body of traditional wheat-bread recipes and an appreciation of good bread that did not decline until the turn of this century.

Likewise, as land in the South became more thickly settled and more of the former open spaces were devoted to cash crops like cotton, the old grazing culture of the South moved west into the Lower Great Plains, where open ranges were readily available. The drover of the eighteenth century, who herded Virginia beef to Baltimore or Philadelphia, a landless workhand whom society held in low esteem, became the "cowboy" of the West. Today there are cookbooks that celebrate his makeshift way of life. He is now one of the most universally stereotyped of all symbols of American folk culture.

It was the "dirt" farmer, however, who contributed most to the various types of breadstuff consumed by early Americans. The specific climate and the agricultural and cultural makeup of each region led to a proliferation of corn-based folk breads.

Bread was the most important food to the folk cook. It took precedence over all other things on the table. Pliny Durant described its position in Clinton County, Ohio, about 1810: "The bread—generally consisting of 'corn pone' or 'corn dodgers' —was baked in a 'skillet' or 'Dutch oven,' or the 'johnny-cake' on a smooth board before the fire. With many, wheat bread and coffee were used on Sabbath mornings."[14] The rest of the week they ate corn bread and drank rye coffee—grains of rye roasted and ground like coffee beans.

The flour of choice was wheat, because white bread was equated with high social status—*any* kind of white food was difficult to make under hearth conditions, because it would discolor very easily on contact with iron equipment or when exposed to smoke and ash. In practice, wheat was a cash crop for most farmers; corn was the grain of use. Furthermore, corn grew in many marginal places where wheat would not. *Middling bread,* or what we now call whole wheat bread, was generally the best grade of wheat bread that most people ever saw at table.

More likely, middling bread was made of wheat flour mixed with rye or cornmeal. This was known as "brown bread" or "rye-and-Indian," and according to the old assize of bread in force in most colonial towns, the proportion of meal and flour in the mix and the weight of each loaf was fixed by law. Because the old laws were rather specific on these points, it is fairly easy to reconstruct a "legal" loaf. All bread, incidentally, was sold by weight, which is why the bakers were given to cheating and why the market sheriff spent so much of his time checking for adulterations and strange ingredients designed to make loaves heavy.

Brown bread was poor man's fare, but in New England it was romanticized in the nineteenth century and equated with old Puritan values and solid Yankee character. Like the cowboy, it thus rose from its position of scorn to become a positive cultural symbol. Boston brown bread is much moister than standard rye-and-Indian, but there are as many recipes as there are opinions as to which is most authentic and which is not.

As a type of bread, Boston brown bread is a very old form of dark bread related to German pumpernickel. Brown bread is half bread, half pudding, and its antecedents, like those of Pennsylvania Dutch Gumbis, are medieval. It is, in the truest sense, a

hearth bread because it is a bread meant to be baked "down hearth," or in the ashes. It was a popular yeoman's bread before brick bread ovens became features of English—and New England—farmhouses in the mid-seventeenth century. It makes wonderful toast.

Brown bread was baked in a deep earthenware dish, a large pattypan glazed on the interior, which was also used for a variety of other things, such as puddings. Puddings made with native fruits, such as whortleberries or huckleberries in New

Thick-crusted rye-and-Indian bread baked six hours in a Dutch oven.

England and persimmons in the Lower Midwest, were highly valued by folk cooks. Long, slow baking was characteristic of this type of cookery, with a loaf of bread or a pudding taking as much as five or six hours to bake. This freed the cook to devote her attention to other tasks around the house.

In the Middle States, where wheat flour was cheaper and more abundant, various types of wheat breads served as the staff of life. Baking in this region was generally done in brick bread ovens set away from the house as protection against fire.

In the South, common folk baked corn bread "down hearth," hence the widespread use of the term *ash cake*. Actually, the bread was not put into the ashes but was spread on a board and set near the fire. When one side was finished baking, the cake or flat bread was turned over to finish on the other side. The large flat cornbreads known as *johnny cakes* were baked in this fashion. Often they were set against metal or wooden driers like the oatcake driers of Scotland and Ireland. The term *hoecake* simply alludes to the fact that the cake or flat bread was propped against a hoe blade to dry rather than against a *branar,* as the drying racks were called.

All of these major regional differences in bread baking were discussed in an article on American breads in the *American Ag-riculturist* in 1873.[15] By that time, traditional bread baking of all kinds was being replaced by "pan breads" (breads baked in tins) and techniques based on the cast-iron stove, a shift that I discuss in greater detail in chapter 5. The important thing to remember is that the old breads were hand-molded, and that in itself was an art.

Corn dodgers, already mentioned, were breads shaped like goose eggs. They were baked either on a griddle or in a dripping pan, the shallow pan that was used to catch drippings from a roast. The hominy bread in the recipe at the end of this chapter was also baked in a dripping pan. Most cooks did not have a large selection of pans in which to bake; thus, implements like the dripping pan were often multifunctional.

The fact that they are baked in a dripping pan does not make corn dodgers any easier to prepare. Of all the hand-molded corn breads, they are among the most resistant to the will of the cook. They are either perfection or disaster. There is no in-between.

Other small breads could be made on a hanging griddle—one of the most versatile hearth implements. These included New England pancakes—such as those in the 1787 recipe provided at the end of this chapter—beaten biscuits, mush muffins—which Connecticut folk referred to as "slipperdown muffins" or just "slipper-downs"—and various kinds of fritters. The drop-dumpling recipe in chapter 1 can be baked on the griddle like fritters. All of these breads could also be baked in a spider.

Spiders were large frying pans with long legs; eighteenth-century spiders also had long handles so that the cook would not be scorched by the fire. In the nineteenth century, the term was transferred to similar pans with short legs and finally to any sort of deep cast-iron skillet. The recipe I have included for spider corn cake preserves this evolution in its name. If pork cracklings (chitlins) were added to the corn bread, it became known as crackling bread, a favorite with many people in the tidewater South.

Just as cracklings gave their distinctive flavor to crackling bread, so did the various cooking fats used in different regions of the country to grease the griddle or dripping

Earthenware pudding pan by Hervey Brooks of Goshen, Connecticut, circa 1840. (Old Sturbridge Village)

Johnny cake drier or branar. *Attributed to John Bailey, New York City, circa 1785. Courtesy of Mr. and Mrs. Kent Gilyard.*

pan. New Englanders generally used pork fat, while Southerners used ham fat.[16] Even if cooks in different parts of the country began with the same corn-bread recipe, the results would be quite different, both in color (because of the different cornmeal preferences) and in underlying flavor.

Before cookbook literature began to scatter recipes far beyond their areas of origin, many of these old American bread forms were quite localized in character. Corn dodgers, for example, were made with unsifted white cornmeal and water in Kentucky. In milk-rich Ohio, they were made with sifted yellow cornmeal that was scalded with milk and thickened with sour cream. Catherine Beecher mentioned these differences in two corn-dodger recipes she published in 1846.[17]

The use of yellow cornmeal by Northerners was always a source of dismay and irritation to Southerners who came to visit, because in the South cornmeal must always be *white*. In 1874 a woman traveling east from Missouri, where Southern preferences prevail, remarked that she could not find any good cornmeal in the country through which she went: "First, they used yellow corn and secondly, their meal was too fine, which makes clammy bread."[18]

Baking bread New England style in a *bake-kettle* or Dutch oven. Woodcut from the *American Agriculturist*. Hot coals went beneath and on top of the Dutch oven.

Baking bread in a detached bakeoven according to practice in the Middle States. Bread is allowed to rise in the rye straw baskets shown in the foreground. Woodcut from the *American Agriculturist*.

MARYLAND BISCUIT

1894

This is the so-called beaten biscuit in which Maryland cooks have a great deal of pride. Mrs. Gibson's directions in the original recipe may seem intimidating: "Beat the dough with an ax for half an hour, until the dough is soft, or until it breaks when pulled. Machines come for this purpose, which facilitate the operation." The machines she was referring to were curious-looking affairs called "biscuit breaks." The simplest kinds, for household use, were generally made of poplar and white oak and featured a wooden mangle with which to work the dough. Each run of the dough through the break was called a "turn." Oral tradition in Maryland often says that for family, the dough requires 300 turns, but for company, it must be 500. You do not need a break or an ax to make Maryland biscuit, but you will need a large rolling pin, a strong arm, and patience.

YIELD: 3 DOZEN BISCUITS.

4 cups pastry flour
¼ pound lard
½ cup milk

½ cup water
2 teaspoons sea salt

Rub the flour and lard through a sieve until the mixture forms a fine crumb. Mix the milk and water and dissolve the salt in it. Pour this over the flour and work it into a stiff dough. Take a heavy rolling pin and beat the dough, folding it from time to time as you would puff pastry. When the dough is spongy and snaps when pulled, it is ready. (Thirty minutes is about the average time it will take to beat the dough to get it to this stage. The break shortens the time by at least half.)

Preheat the oven to 425°F.

The biscuits may be formed in two ways: by hand or with a tin cutter. If doing them by hand, form balls of dough about the size of a walnut (they should weigh about 1 ounce). Knead them so that they are smooth on the top, then set them on greased baking sheets. Roll them lightly with a rolling pin to flatten the tops, then prick them with a fork.

If using a tin cutter, roll the entire batch of dough to a thickness of ½ inch. Then cut out 2-inch rounds with a cutter. Set these on greased baking sheets and prick with a fork. Bake the biscuits in the pre-heated oven for 15 minutes. They should be lightly colored on top, white on the sides, and pale golden on the bottom.

SOURCE. Marietta P. Gibson. *Mrs. Charles H. Gibson's Maryland and Virginia Cook Book.* (Baltimore: John Murphy & Co., 1894), 17.

Maryland biscuit *break* and beaten biscuits. In the foreground on the right, tin and wood biscuit *docks* from the nineteenth century.

Earthenware tart dish, Rhode Island, circa 1780–
1820. Courtesy of the Henry Francis du Pont
Winterthur Museum.

BOILED CIDER PIE

ca. 1865

YIELD: TWO 8-INCH PIES.

4 tablespoons all-purpose flour
1 cup cold water
2 egg yolks
½ cup plain, unsweetened apple butter ("boiled cider")

1 cup dark brown sugar
1 teaspoon cinnamon
½ teaspoon nutmeg
2 prebaked 8-inch pie shells

Mix the flour and cold water and beat until completely smooth and free of lumps. In a separate bowl, beat the egg yolks, then add the apple butter, sugar, flour-water mixture, and spices. Put the batter in a double boiler and whisk until it thickens and begins to set. Pour it into the 2 pre-baked, 8-inch pie shells. Carefully brown the tops under the broiler. (The old method was to use a heated salamander.) If you are worried about scorching the crusts, set the pies instead in an oven pre-heated to 350°F, allowing 5 to 8 minutes for them to brown.

In addition, you may ornament the tops of the pies with a meringue made from the egg whites. The design shown here, from an 1884 wood engraving, was piped on with an icing bag and looks very good against the dark brown filling. If the pies are decorated with meringue, return them to the oven for a few minutes in order for the meringues to set.

SOURCE: Mrs. E. F. Sargent, Manuscript Cookbook. (Walpole, New Hampshire, ca. 1865). Roughwood Collection.

OVERLEAF: *Interior of the Steamboat Princess* by Marie Adrien Persac (1861). Courtesy of the Anglo-American Art Museum, Louisiana State University, Baton Rouge.

HOMINY BREAD

1870

This recipe produces a form of spoon bread that can be sliced and served hot. It has a delightful texture. Another version reduces the milk by half and results in something akin to a moist pound cake. When cooked rice is substituted for the hominy, the dish is sometimes called Mississippi corn bread. All of these variations were served on the steamboats that plied the Ohio and Mississippi rivers.

YIELD: 6 TO 8 SERVINGS.

½ cup grits (see note)
2 cups boiling water
1¼ teaspoons salt
1 tablespoon unsalted butter
2 eggs

2 cups old-style "rich" milk
(1½ cups milk mixed with
½ cup cream)
1 cup fine white cornmeal

Preheat the oven to 375°F.

Cook the grits in the boiling water with ¼ teaspoon of the salt until well done (see note). Measure out 2 cups while still warm, and beat in the butter and the remaining teaspoon of salt. Beat the eggs to a froth, then add the milk. Beat this into the hominy to form a batter. Thicken with the cornmeal and pour into a hot, greased baking pan (see note). Put the pan in the oven and immediately turn the oven down to 350°F. Bake for approximately 70 minutes, or until the center has firmly set (see note).

NOTE:

The average cooking time for old-style grits or small hominy is roughly 45 minutes; for quick grits it is about 5 minutes. Cooking time and the amount of hominy needed to make 2 cups will vary greatly, as grits are processed differently in different parts of the country. Please refer to instructions on the package you are using.

I tested this recipe in a round, 10-inch dripping pan with 2½-inch sides. Any baking pan of similar dimension will do.

If you want to make the drier version of this bread, by reducing the milk and cream by half, keep in mind that baking time will also be reduced by half. "Rich" milk is necessary in this recipe because it makes a cheeselike skin on the surface of the bread.

SOURCE: Mrs. T. L. Langston. Manuscript Cookbook. (Atlanta, Georgia, October 28, 1870), 3. Roughwood Collection.

PERSIMMON PUDDING

1915

YIELD: 6 SERVINGS.

¾ cup all-purpose flour
1 teaspoon baking powder
1½ teaspoons powdered cinnamon
1½ teaspoons powdered cloves
2 eggs
2 cups milk

2 cups pureed persimmons (about 10–12 persimmons)
4 tablespoons unsalted butter, softened
¾ cup sugar (or more to taste)

Preheat the oven to 450°F.

Sift together the flour, baking powder, and spices. In a separate bowl, beat the eggs to a froth, then combine with the milk. Beat the pureed persimmon and butter together to form a batter, then beat in the milk and eggs. Add the sugar and adjust the sweetness. (This will depend largely on the ripeness of the persimmons.) Sift in the dry ingredients and beat until the batter is smooth and free of lumps.

Pour mixture into a greased baking dish, preferably one about 12 × 9 × 2. Bake for 15 minutes, then reduce heat to 400°F and bake for 25 to 30 minutes, or until the pudding is set in the center and pulling away from the sides of the baking dish.

NOTE:

Persimmon pudding has all the fickleness of a soufflé. Do not start baking it until you are certain you can serve it as soon as it is done. It is also easy to scorch.

Pyrex baking dishes bake much hotter than earthenware, so baking time may be 5 to 10 minutes shorter than given above. Also, persimmon pulp can be made up and frozen while persimmons are in season (October/November). Frozen pulp seems to require more sugar than fresh, especially if wild persimmons are used.

SOURCE: Julia Ellison, ed. *Cook Book Compiled by the Members of "The Sojourner's Club."* (Kirksville, Missouri: Journal Printing Company, 1915), 127.

BOSTON BROWN BREAD
1873

Genuine Boston brown bread is a species of baked pudding not too different from old-fashioned rye-and-Indian, another coarse New England bread. And like rye-and-Indian, the basic recipe is both the picture of simplicity and extremely difficult to get right. One of the problems today is commercial cornmeal, which is too dense; another is the yeast, which can sour cornmeal all too easily. I have adjusted the recipe to compensate for this, so follow my directions explicitly and do *not* use an exotic, old-fashioned grade of cornmeal. Use common supermarket cornmeal.

The ideal pan is a deep 2-quart cast-iron pattypan. Lacking that, a charlotte mold will work as well, provided it is set in a pan of water while baking and that you can procure a tight-fitting lid. Some people use pudding tins with center tubes; that kind of pan willl also do.

YIELD: 10 TO 12 SERVINGS.

1 cup whole wheat flour
3 cups plus 2 tablespoons fine
yellow cornmeal
1½ cups rye flour
1 teaspoon sea salt
½ cup unsulfured molasses

Approximately 5 cups boiling water
½ cup very active yeast (¼ ounce
yeast proofed in ¼ cup warm water
with ¼ cup molasses)
Lard or bacon drippings

Sift the whole wheat flour to remove most of the bran. Mix the flour with the cornmeal, rye flour, and salt in a large mixing bowl. Make a well in the center and add the molasses. Scald this with the boiling water and beat the batter until smooth. If it is too stiff, add more hot water. Allow the batter to cool.

When the yeast has developed a head like beer, add it to the batter and beat well. Using lard or bacon drippings, liberally grease the interior of a 2-quart pan with slanting sides. Add the batter, which should fill the pan two-thirds full.

Cover tightly and let the batter rise in a warm place until it comes to within half an inch of the top (about two hours). Then set the pan in an oven preheated to 375°F for 15 minutes. Turn the heat down to 325°F and bake for another 75 to 85 minutes. During baking, the bread will shrink somewhat and pull away from the sides of the pan. It will develop a heavy brown crust and a gray-brown crumb.

NOTE:

The old method, using large earthenware pans, required a very low, steady heat—about 275°F—for 5½ to 6 hours.

SOURCE: William H. Tutt. *Dr. Tutt's Manual of Valuable Information and Useful Receipts.* (New York: Dr. William H. Tutt, 1873.)

MUSH MUFFINS

1915

This is the recipe of Josephine Rakestraw, a close friend of my grandmother's aunt and a member of Marlborough Friends Meeting near Unionville, Pennsylvania. Mush muffins were considered very "old-fashioned" when her recipe was published.

This was also the first bread recipe I learned to make on an open hearth—my grandmother instructing. As fast as we baked them, Abigail, Granny's dog, grabbed the hot muffins off the griddle. YIELD: 2 DOZEN 3-INCH MUFFINS.

1 quart cooked small yellow hominy
(see note)
2 cups lukewarm milk
1 tablespoon lard or unsalted butter

1 tablespoon sea salt
¼ cup warm water in which
¼ ounce yeast has been proofed
10–10½ cups bread or hard flour

While the hominy is still warm, beat in the milk, lard, and salt. When it is tepid, add the proofed yeast. Then gradually sift in only enough flour to form a dough that is no longer tacky to handle. Knead 10 minutes, dusting occasionally with flour if necessary. Cover and set aside to proof overnight, or until double in bulk.

Preheat the oven to 375°F.

Punch down the dough and dust the work surface with flour. Roll out dough to a thickness of 1 inch and cut out 3-inch rounds. Set them on greased baking sheets and let rise for 15 minutes. Then bake for approximately 20 minutes.

N O T E :

The cooking time and the amount of hominy needed to make 1 quart of mush will vary greatly, as grits are processed differently in different parts of the country. Please refer to instructions on the package you are using.

SOURCE: East Marlboro Branch of County Auxiliary. *Our Favorite Recipes.* (Kennett Square, Pa.: privately printed, 1915), 34.

Waterman muffin pan with Mush Muffins.

Corn Dodgers

1889

Corn dodgers are muffins or "pones" the size and shape of goose eggs. The trick is to use as little liquid as possible when making up the dough. The griddle must be extremely hot, and the dough should come in contact with the griddle in an area no larger than a quarter—at most, a tablespoon. Some say it should just "kiss" the griddle. This means, of course, that your cornmeal must be as stiff as mashed potatoes—a crucial point.

YIELD: APPROXIMATELY 12 DODGERS.

4 cups fine yellow cornmeal
1 tablespoon lard or unsalted butter
2 cups water
1 teaspoon salt

2 eggs
Milk (only if necessary)
Lard or bacon drippings

Mix the cornmeal and lard with your fingers. Bring the water to a boil, dissolve the salt in it, and scald the cornmeal. When the cornmeal is lukewarm, beat the eggs and work them into the cornmeal. If the cornmeal is too dry (falling apart), moisten it with milk. (It should hold together like mashed potatoes.) Let it stand for 15 to 20 minutes while the griddle is heating.

When the griddle is hot, grease it well with lard or bacon drippings (the latter is more authentic), and form the cornmeal into goose-egg-shaped balls, using 2 large spoons. Gently set the dodgers on the griddle, and bake until the bottoms are golden brown and the interiors are steaming hot. Serve immediately like English muffins. When cold, these are excellent toasted.

SOURCE: Ladies of the First Presbyterian Church. *Presbyterian Cook Book.* (Wheeling, West Virginia: F. H. Crago, 1889), 105.

VINEGAR PIE

The popular cookbook from which this recipe is taken was first published in Detroit in 1882. Many of the recipes come from the Midwest. This recipe might be called "Poor Man's Lemon Meringue Pie," because that is precisely what it makes with the zest of only half a lemon. In fact, it makes four pies.

YIELD: FOUR 6½–7-INCH PIES, OR TWO 9-INCH PIES.

1½ cups cider vinegar
2 cups water
4 tablespoons unsalted butter
1½ cups plus 2 teaspoons sugar
Zest of ½ lemon

5 eggs, separated
3 tablespoons all-purpose flour
Four 6½–7-inch pie shells, or two
9-inch pie shells

Preheat the oven to 325°F.

Heat the vinegar, 1 cup of the water, butter, the 1½ cups of sugar, and lemon zest in a saucepan. Beat the egg yolks with the remaining cup of water and flour until smooth. As the vinegar boils, whisk in the egg-and-flour mixture and continue whisking until it thickens. Pour the filling into unbaked pie shells and bake in the preheated oven for 35 to 40 minutes, or until the filling sets. When done, remove the pies from the oven and beat the egg whites until stiff. Sweeten with the remaining 2 teaspoons sugar and spread over the pies. Return them to the oven and brown the meringue for 10 minutes. Then remove the pies and set aside to cool. Serve cold.

SOURCE: Mahlon W. Ellsworth and F. B. Dickerson. *The Successful Housekeeper.* (Harrisburg, Pa.: Pennsylvania Publishing Co., 1883), 138.

SPIDER CORN CAKE
1887

A spider is an old-fashioned term for a long-handled frying pan that stands on three legs. This recipe was created in the 1820s or 1830s to take advantage of commercial cast-iron spiders. Baking was accomplished by pushing hot coals under the pan and scattering them over the lid. The result is a luscious form of corn bread.

YIELD: 6 SERVINGS.

1⅔ cups white cornmeal (see note)
⅓ cup whole wheat flour
¼ cup granulated sugar
1 teaspoon salt
1 teaspoon baking soda

2 eggs
1 cup buttermilk
2 tablespoons unsalted butter
1 cup rich milk (made by mixing
⅔ cup milk with ⅓ cup cream)

Sift together the cornmeal, flour, sugar, salt, and baking soda. Beat the eggs to a froth, then beat in the buttermilk. Combine the dry and liquid ingredients.

While making the batter, heat a 10-inch iron spider, or a modern-style skillet, in an oven preheated to 375°F. When the skillet is hot, remove it from the oven, melt the butter in it, and coat the inside of the pan. Add the batter and spread it evenly. Then pour *over* this the cup of rich milk. Do not stir or disturb the batter underneath.

Set the pan in the oven and bake 25 to 30 minutes, or until the cake tests dry in the center. Serve warm as a tea cake.

NOTE:

New-style, processed cornmeal is denser than old-fashioned varieties. It is therefore necessary to remove about 2 ounces for each pound of meal in order to use old cornmeal recipes with success. If you are using processed cornmeal, remove 3½ level tablespoons from the above recipe.

SOURCE: Maria Parloa. *Miss Parloa's Kitchen Companion.* (Boston: Estes and Lauriat, 1887), 805.

NEW ENGLAND PANCAKES
1787

Among high-church people in the South, the old custom for Shrove Monday was egg and callops (bacon or thin pieces of ham), followed by cockfights and pancakes on Shrove Tuesday, and fritters on Wednesday. In New England, the Puritans looked with disfavor on such customs and fully abstained from Lent. But that did not disqualify them from Shrove Tuesday fare under other guises, as this remarkably good recipe attests. Today we would call these little sinners "dessert crepes." They eat well with strawberry preserves.

YIELD: APPROXIMATELY 2½ DOZEN LARGE PANCAKES.

4 eggs plus 3 egg yolks
2 cups heavy cream
½ teaspoon salt
10 tablespoons all-purpose flour

Approximately 4 tablespoons lightly salted butter (for frying)
Sugar and powdered cinnamon

Beat the eggs and yolks together until very light. Then add the cream and salt and beat again until smooth. Gradually sift in the flour until a rich, ropy batter is formed. Beat from time to time while frying the pancakes, to keep the batter light.

Melt a little butter on a hot griddle and spoon some batter into small 6-inch pancakes, or into large ones. Allow about 1 tablespoon of batter for each small cake, 5 tablespoons for each large one. When they are golden brown on one side, flip them over and brown the other. Mason suggested scattering sugar and cinnamon on them. Whatever topping you choose, these pancakes are at their best when warm from the griddle.

SOURCE: Charlotte Mason. *The Ladies' Assistant for Regulating and Supplying the Table.* (London: J. Walter, 1787), 388.

OPPOSITE PAGE: **Tossing the pancake, from an 1837 engraving. (Roughwood Collection)**

Detail of *Salem Common on Training Day* by George Ropes (1808).
The booths in the foreground are selling cakes and beverages.
Courtesy of The Essex Institute.

Recently there has been a movement in the folk-art world to redefine what is meant by the term *folk*. Some writers in Europe have discarded the word in favor of *popular*. A number of Americans have chosen the word *plain*, now referring to folk art as plain art. Folk cookery, however, is composed of so many complex elements that it becomes the ultimate testing ground of terms like these. In the case of *plain*, we are faced with a number of difficulties.

The language of the folk cook has been fairly consistent over the past two centuries about the meaning of *plain*. *Plain cooking*, a common cookbook phrase, was not folk cookery. It was economical cookery, cookery stripped down to basics. It meant frugal, more for less. It was the unpainted box selling for one dollar—plain, as opposed to the painted box selling for three —fancy. It was training cake made with molasses (plain: no sugar, no eggs), as opposed to Salem fancy cake made with white sugar, eggs, and butter. Both were Training Day cookies, the recipes for

which are included at the end of this chapter. One was cheap, one was not.

Plain cookery in this sense is symbolized in the roughcast frugality of the Long Island kitchen depicted in the Thomas Hicks painting at the beginning of this book. Hicks calls attention to the simple luxury of fresh quinces on the table, and for those who know quinces, this hints at their honeylike odor pervading the room, a room opened to the out-of-doors, warmed by the October sun. In short, the artist has made a visual comment about food, folk cookery, and the complex emotional thing called connectedness. In this case, the kitchen and nature overlap.

There is yet another meaning of *plain* that appears in early American cookery, as in Quaker or Shaker plainness, a sectarian expression of restraint. This type of plainness was a conscious editing out of detail, decoration, or of certain tastes and foods that conflicted with a theological point of view. It was a plainness embraced by many American religious groups, even by Methodists and Presbyterians, since in the nineteenth century the idea of plainness, of withdrawal from worldly corruption, was an acceptable alternative life-style among those who had "come to Christ." The woman in the Hicks painting is not a Quaker, but she is dressed plainly in this sectarian sense, and this adds yet another level of meaning to the scene—something a nineteenth-century viewer would have recognized immediately.

We also know, historically speaking, that plainness, even among Quakers, was a relatively recent development, beginning in earnest about 1800. As is the case with the Amish of today, plainness of costume did not necessarily carry over into all other aspects of their culture—an important point when it comes to cookery.

Lewis Mumford, in the quote at the beginning of this book, referred to plain cooking in still another sense—as a form of honest food, undeceptive, the very best of its sort. This approaches the kind of home cookery aimed for by Elizabeth Lea in her *Domestic Cookery,* mentioned earlier. It was a cookery that aimed for organic goodness built up through high-quality ingredients and direct, uncomplicated techniques. Without saying so, without expounding on culinary theory, Elizabeth Lea gave order and principle to her folk cookery, the sort of cookery Lewis Mumford knew and understood. Trained in architecture, Mumford was fully sensitive to organic structure—to things designed from the inside out, forms that followed purpose, houses that fit people, food that filled.

Plainness, in all of these meanings—frugality, moral restraint, and honesty of ingredients—is continuously at work in folk cookery, just as it is in folk art. And it shapes the two largest branches of folk expression: the art of work and the art of leisure. This complexity of plainness, especially in connection with cookery for leisure, is easiest to see in the molasses training cake, which was plain in structure but often elaborately ornamented. This "double play" allowed folk cooks to invent an extraordinary range of recipes that stayed within given limitations, such as cost or religious scruples, yet gave vent to remarkable creative instincts. One could say that it was a cookery both effusive and highly controlled. In this respect, it borrowed the mannerisms of eighteenth-century music.

In the following pages, we will explore three examples of early American festive cookery to illustrate this: cakes for the militia muster, or Election (or Training) Day as it was called, funeral biscuits, and ornamented New Year's cakes. The first was cookery for a public celebration, the second addressed the life cycle, and the third was calendrical. In all of these cases, the structure of the special food—the complexity of flavor and texture—was subordinated to its symbolic purpose.

Trooping in the Cakes

In the Colonial period, each region of the country had its own feasts connected with public events. In the Middle States, the sittings of the courts; May Day, when country boys decorated their heads with animal fur and went about the town shooting off guns; and fair days for the semi-annual markets were focal points for great social gatherings and considerable drinking.

At the market fair held in Frederick, Maryland, in April 1747, there were even competitive games such as horse racing on old nags, chasing pigs with soaped tails, and grinning for cheese.[1] The cheese competition was open only to old men and women. The contestant with the ugliest, most toothless grin won the cheese. This custom lingers with us today in the habit of saying "cheese" when we have our picture taken.

Cheese prizes were not the only foods associated with fair days. Gingerbreads, honey cakes, fancy wafers, waffles, funnel cakes, pies, and street foods of every shape and species were hawked by vendors and housewives alike.

Great bonfires were built, and it was not unusual for one of the leading gentlemen in the community to organize an ox roast or bear roast, or "barbecue," as open-air roasting was then called. The high cost of such largesse was underwritten by the host as part of the obligation of his social position. In the shifting struggle for power and status, it was a good way to acquire "friends."

After the Revolution, when many market fairs were discontinued because of the attendant rowdiness and disorder, the outdoor roasting customs were transferred to political rallies. At the presidential campaign rally for Harrison and Tyler held at Wilmington, Ohio, in 1840, 1,000 people gathered to raise a log cabin and consume corn dodgers, hard cider, and barbecued ham.[2] The Harrison and Tyler campaign made a concerted effort to portray the can-

Wafer irons with the great seal of the United States, circa 1845. Courtesy of Hazel Marcus.

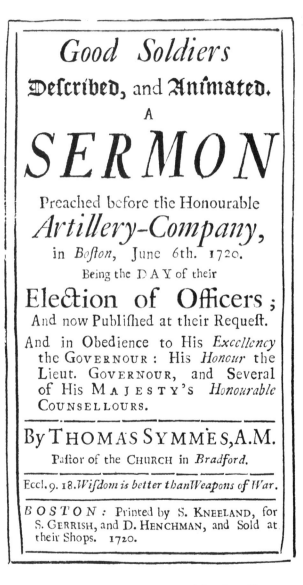

Good Soldiers
𝕯𝖊𝖘𝖈𝖗𝖎𝖇𝖊𝖉, and 𝖆𝖓𝖎𝖒𝖆𝖙𝖊𝖉.

A

SERMON

Preached before the Honourable
Artillery-Company,
in *Bofton,* June 6th. 1720.

Being the D A Y of their

Election of Officers ;

And now Publifhed at their Requeft.

And in Obedience to His *Excellency*
the GOVERNOUR : His *Honour* the
Lieut. GOVERNOUR, and Several
of His MAJESTY'S *Honourable*
COUNSELLOURS.

By THOMAS SYMMES, A.M.

Paftor of the CHURCH in *Bradford.*

Eccl. 9. 18. *Wifdom is better than Weapons of War.*

BOSTON : Printed by S. KNEELAND, for
S. GERRISH, and D. HENCHMAN, and Sold at
their Shops. 1720.

Rare Election Day sermon printed for the officers
of the Boston militia. Courtesy of Mr. and Mrs.
James Gergat.

didates as down-to-earth frontier heroes, friends of the farmer and the working man. That is why corn dodgers and other patriotic folk foods were served to the voters. American politicians have relied on this formula ever since.[3]

In New England, the situation was somewhat different, because of Congregationalist attitudes about public feasting. In general, public events were tied in some fashion to the church, which thus exerted an influence over their character. One of the most important of these events was the election of officers of the various county militias. This normally took place around the end of May and gave Congregationalists a spring counterpart to Thanksgiving and a substitute for Easter.

Election Day, or Training Day (its other name), provided the militia with an occasion to parade. It gave the local minister an excuse to sermonize. And it gave the community a happy day of leisure filled with cake, gingerbread, drinking, and socializing about the town common. Such a militia exercise held at Salem, Massachusetts, in 1808 has been recorded in minute detail by the folk painter George Ropes. In the foreground, around the edge of Salem Common, he showed the tents and booths set up to sell beverages and cakes.

The raised cakes made with yeast that were served at these events were called "election cakes" by New Englanders. The cookies, usually some type of crisp gingerbread, were called "training cakes." Training cakes were often stamped or decorated with wooden "prints," as the carved molds were formerly called. The motifs on training cakes were generally secular and usually patriotic. Before the Revolution, they often depicted coats of arms of the governor, King George, or an Indian. After the Revolution, the American eagle became one of the most popular motifs. Indian figures also remained popular, but with reference to the Boston Tea Party.

Lucy Larcom, in her *New England Girlhood* (1889), described Election Day as she remembered it from her childhood in Beverly, Massachusetts:

> "Old Election," " 'Lection Day" we called it, a lost holiday now, was a general training day, and it came at our most delightful season, the last of May. Lilacs and tulips were in bloom, then; and it was a picturesque fashion of the time for little girls whose parents had no flower-gardens to go around begging a bunch of lilacs, or a tulip or two. My mother always made " 'Lection cake" for us on that day. It was nothing but a kind of sweetened bread with a shine of egg-and-molasses on top; but we thought it delicious.[4]

Election cake and training cake were not specific recipes, but generic names, like "picnic cake." Both cakes often went by other labels, in many cases taking their name from the town where that particular recipe was in vogue. Norwich raised cake (from Norwich, Connecticut) and Worcester loaf (from Worcester, Massachusetts, and baked in a turk's-cap mold) were two very popular election-cake recipes. The most famous of the election cakes was the Hartford recipe. The oldest recipe, however, is the one I have included in this book. It comes from Boston.

After the 1830s militia fairs began to fall out of fashion in New England, and election cake was sometimes shifted to serve other social functions. Thus, old things acquired new guises, as in camp meeting cake and Massasoit loaf cake, a cake served at parties commemorating the Pilgrims.

Colonial Revival iron cookie stamp depicting Washington giving his Farewell Address, circa 1865.

A Biscuit for Remembrance

Funeral entertainments, like militia fairs, were accorded a place of considerable importance in colonial America. In the small rural communities that typified much of the eastern United States by the late eighteenth century, the custom of lavish dining at the house of mourning—or in a nearby tavern—was firmly established. While the feasting varied in format from region to region and from one religious denomination to another, there were certain features that linked them all to common Old World funeral practices. Perhaps the most significant of these was the funeral token, something distributed to the mourners as a reminder of the lately departed.

Funeral tokens assumed many forms. In New England, gifts of white mourning gloves were common from the seventeenth century on. Elsewhere, the token might consist of a broadside sermon, a copy of the hymn sung at graveside, elegiac verses, or, if the estate of the deceased permitted, religious pamphlets on the theme of salvation. The most ephemeral token, however, was the funeral biscuit, which took its place among a long list of entertainment foods on the funeral menu. Because it was ornamented, often with highly symbolic motifs, the funeral biscuit was, in the most literal sense, edible folk art.

Historical references to funeral biscuits and the carved wooden stamps used to make them are at best skimpy, undoubtedly because the custom was so commonplace that it was hardly news in early letters and accounts. An entry from the diary of Virginia planter William Byrd typifies the offhand manner in which the funeral biscuit was treated. On June 26, 1712, after attending services for his deceased friend Captain Llewellyn, Byrd noted: "We had wine and biscuits according to custom."[5]

Byrd lived on a plantation in a neighborhood that was not conveniently close to a large town. Captain Llewellyn's biscuits could have been sent out from Williamsburg, but more likely, they were baked locally by one of the women in the community. The most obvious person would be the wife of the minister, since funerals were in her husband's line of work. But the wife of the coffin maker might also bake them, or even someone in the home of the deceased. In rural communities, such molds were scarce and often lent out, circulating as the need arose from household to household.

The most popular of all motifs on English and American funeral biscuits was the heart. A walnut mold with a heart design from Virginia's Eastern Shore is shown on the back cover of this book. The heart is also the most ancient of the decorative devices found in funeral cookery, predating Christianity. Other designs might include a cherub or winged head—symbolizing the spirit of the deceased rising to heaven—an hourglass, or even a skull.

One of the rarest and most unusual of these designs can be seen in a Cohee mold of poplar depicting stylized dwarf thistles (*Carduus pumilus*). Dating from about 1815, it comes from central Pennsylvania, where the dwarf thistle is common in old fields. The reddish-purple flower is highly fragrant—a characteristic of mourning flowers—and its flower head is larger than those of other American thistles. This is why it is often confused in folk art for a tulip. The flower buds are so large, in fact, that they were often cooked and eaten like artichokes.

Nineteenth-century flower books usually depict the thistle as a symbol of austerity and, by association, of plainness and

Cohee funeral biscuit stamp.
(Philadelphia Museum of Art)

restraint.[6] But it is not likely that the symbolism in this case can be found in popular literature. Rather, it is more likely to be found in the folklore peculiar to the Scotch-Irish origins of the community that produced this mold.

In larger cities, such as Philadelphia, where there was a thriving biscuit trade, some bakers specialized in funeral cookery, since they could depend on a steady flow of business. Benjamin Betterton, for example, advertised in the *Pennsylvania Journal* for February 9, 1748, that he offered a line of "Burial Biscake"—*biscake* being an old American folk term for *cookie*. Bakers like Betterton had access to first-rate woodcarvers and could therefore afford to use more elaborate molds. City clientele also demanded more sophisticated or fashionable designs.

A rare Philadelphia mold from about 1785 depicts three plumes. The plumes refer not to the insignia of the Prince of Wales, but to the black plumes decorating the corners of a hearse and worn by the horses pulling it. Another mold has been located from the same workshop depicting an elaborately carved rooster, a symbol of resurrection and a popular motif on early American funeral biscuits.

Peter Brears of the University of Leeds in England has undertaken considerable work on funeral biscuits in northern York-shire. In the Yorkshire Dales, funeral biscuits took the form of round shortbreads stamped with four-inch prints.[7] Most of the recipes are flavored with caraway seeds. In Lincolnshire, "seed bread," another species of funeral fare, was also flavored with caraway seeds, or even tansy seeds.[8] Both caraway and tansy were used in colonial America.

The oldest known funeral-biscuit recipe preserved in the United States is one found in the 1702 household memorandum book of Samuel Nutt, an early Pennsylvania iron master. This recipe is included at the end of this chapter. Oddly enough, it appeared many years later under the name of "Hard Gingerbread" in Caroline Gilman's *Lady's Annual Register* (Boston, 1838)—the same Caroline Gilman of Roseland Plantation mentioned in chapter 1.[9]

Philadelphia biscuit mold (*opposite page*) and the decorated biscuit made with it (*above*).

Because of our climate, we tend to make our biscuits and gingerbreads much harder than the English or continental Europeans. The lines of distinction between American molasses shortbreads and gingerbreads grew blurred at an early date. It is fairly evident from common practice that most "hard" gingerbreads could also serve as funeral biscuits, provided that caraway or tansy seeds were added. Caraway in particular seems to have been a requisite flavor. It did not matter that the biscuits were hard because they were meant to be dipped in fruit wine or in beer or ale, which is what the men were generally served.

As for serving funeral biscuits, it would be useful to know what William Byrd meant by "according to custom" in his 1712 remark. Explanations for tantalizing comments like that can sometimes be found elsewhere. Among the Lutherans of Montgomery County, Pennsylvania, "according to custom" meant this:

> The daughter of a principal farmer was selected, who took a large pewter plate, laden with bread and cakes, and stationed herself on the side of the path by which the procession was to pass from the church to the grave. A young man, son of one of the farmers of the first class, held a large plate, upon which was a bottle of wine or whisky and a wine cup, and took position opposite the young woman. Each person in passing took a piece of bread or cake from the maiden, and then turned to the other side and took a sip of wine from the cup, which the youth replenished from time to time.[10]

The bread and "cakes" referred to are the funeral bread (sweetened with sugar or honey and containing caraway seeds or

Roller mold by John Conger (1827–1835). Courtesy of the Henry Francis du Pont Winterthur Museum.

dried fruit) and the biscuits discussed above. Early in the eighteenth century, the Pennsylvania Dutch acquired the habit of serving funeral biscuits from their English-speaking neighbors.

In New York City, John Conger, who worked between 1827 and 1835, was one of the best-known of all American mold carvers. He made an unusual roller mold about 1835 depicting sprigs of roses, which is now in the collection of the Henry Francis du Pont Winterthur Museum in Delaware. The rose, as a funeral motif, grew increasingly popular in the Victorian period. It often symbolized a child who had died young, a theme explained in pathetic detail in the following elegiac poem published in 1890 after the death of little Raymond McCool, aged six months and twenty-three days.[11]

Marble funeral biscuit stamp, Schenectady, New York, circa 1840–1870.

> *A bud the Gardener gave us,*
> *A fine and lovely child;*
> *He gave it to our keeping*
> *To cherish undefiled.*
> *But just as it was opening*
> *In the glory of the day*
> *Down came the Heavenly Gardener*
> *And took our bud away.*

The sprig of budding rose, snipped from the bush, is of course an apt image for untimely death, but the allusion goes much deeper than that, since Christ himself was cut off at an early age. He is also called "the Rose of Sharon" (Song of Solomon 2:1), and therefore, the rose, like the rooster, is implicitly a symbol of resurrection.

The powerful religious implications of this image blend in a strange and somewhat haunting way in the marble biscuit molds carved in the Schenectady area of upstate New York from about 1840 to 1870. The motifs on these molds are the same as those used in local gravestone art. The pictorial and psychological relationship between food art and gravestone art is not accidental.

Eventually, the rose displaced most of the other motifs as a funeral-cake symbol. And in an attempt to give a Christian connotation to the otherwise secular American New Year's celebration, the rose, as a symbol of renewal and hope, was extended in evangelical literature to include imagery of the newborn year. This is evident in an 1878 New Year's card that depicts a spray of roses laid across an open hymn book of the oblong sort formerly used in Sunday schools and camp meeting revivals.

The appeal of the rose as an image of rebirth and renewal grew with the evangelical movement in this country. But as evangelism also brought with it Temperance, funeral feasting was gradually reorganized along more restricted lines. Thus,

by the late nineteenth century, the funeral biscuit, now replaced by multitudes of bake-sale goods—from scripture cake to divinity fudge—became a relic of a more indulgent past.

A Rose for New Year's

In a little essay called "New Year's Day in New York," Tyrone Power described his experience on New Year's Day 1834: "On this day, from early hour, every door in New York is open, and all the good things possessed by the inmates paraded in lavish profusion."[12] Among that lavish profusion of edibles were the ornamented New Year's cakes for which the city was justly famous.

The American New Year's cake originated in New York, and like "election cake" and "training cake," the name covered a broad range of recipes. For the most part, however, the New Year's cake was white. It sometimes contained caraway seeds, sometimes powdered coriander or cardamom. It could be made plain and be cut in rounds or squares like the recipe in Amelia Simmons's *American Cookery* of 1796.[13]

It could also be ornamented with cake "prints." The smallest molds were used in the home for the *koekje* ("little cakes"),

Chromolithograph New Year's card dated 1878.
(Roughwood Collection)

from which our present-day term *cookie* is derived. The largest and most elaborate molds were used by bakers, hotels, and shopkeepers to make display pieces for their windows on New Year's Day.

The custom of making New Year's cakes came to New York in the seventeenth century with the New Netherlands Dutch, whose descendants kept alive the custom and gradually passed it on to their English-speaking neighbors. By the end of the eighteenth century, when New York City served as the capital of the United States, New Year's cakes were in vogue among upper-class Americans, who imitated the New York custom of open-house visiting on New Year's Day. Since New Year's cake molds had no specific religious connotations, even plain groups like the Quakers found them acceptable. And since neither Quakers nor Congregationalists celebrated Christmas, the New Year's cake offered them a theologically "safe" alternative. For this reason, New Year's cake recipes spread quickly among these two groups. The recipe at the end of this chapter is taken from the manuscript cookbook of a Long Island Quaker.

New York City became a center for the production of New Year's cake molds, and several different schools of carving evolved by the early nineteenth century. The workshop of John Conger, already mentioned, produced many large, elaborate molds, usually in mahogany. Conger generally repeated stock motifs over and over in slightly different arrangements in the thousands of molds that his shop produced. This is easily seen when several Conger molds are placed side by side. Some molds, however, were made as commission pieces to commemorate specific events, and their designs are generally one of a kind. Conger also made rolling pins from scrap mahogany to go with his large molds. They were probably sold together as a working unit.

Conger's method of work was to lay out his design with a compass and trace off patterns from his set repertoire. These included Indians, American soldiers, Scottish dancers, the American eagle, a bird in a basket, and a variety of floral and cornucopia motifs that also appear on New York furniture of the same period. This has led to speculation that Conger may have worked as a carver for Duncan Phyfe or other shops of that caliber. There may be some foundation to this, since Conger did work for a time as a furniture carver in Philadelphia. He is one of the few documented carvers of New York cake prints who both produced the molds and retailed New Year's cakes.

OPPOSITE PAGE: Square Conger cake print showing his popular Scottish motifs—dancers, barley sheaf, thistles, hops, and wild rose. (Old Sturbridge Village)

New Year Cake Prints,
ROLLERS,
SPRINGLER FORMS,
JELLY MOULDS,
Copper Pans,
FURNACES, &c.

☞ *Every Tool necessary for Bakers, Confectioners, Restaurants and Hotels.*

WILLIAM HART, Manufacturer,
No. 34 CATHARINE STREET, NEW YORK.

Rare cake print advertisement from *The Confectioners' Journal*, December 1876.

Other New York carvers, such as William Hart, produced large, elaborate molds, and many of them are mistakenly assigned to Conger. There were professional carvers working in Albany, New York; New Brunswick, New Jersey; Philadelphia; New Castle and Wilmington, Delaware; and Baltimore. There were also hundreds of homemade pieces carved by rural furniture makers, gravestone cutters, and by young men who made them as presentation pieces to their girlfriends, or to their relatives, such as a sister or mother.

Conger's successor in the New York mold trade was the firm of James Y. Watkins, which specialized in kitchen furnishings and remained in business into this century. Watkins subcontracted its mold work to a variety of carvers. The firm's mark, which often appears on pieces retailed from the store, indicates only that Watkins sold it. And since Watkins bought out the old Conger stock, many Conger molds also bear the Watkins stamp.

Watkins was responsible for the continued manufacture of Conger designs until at least 1900, and in 1899, the firm is known to have issued a catalogue of "cake print" patterns for the baking trade.[14] These later molds were usually stamped with a pattern number, and all of them were done by the same machine stamp-and-gouge process used at the time to mass-produce molds for Springerle cookies.

The Springerle cookie is the German first cousin of the early American New Year's cake. Both cookies share a common seventeenth-century origin in that they are "water" marzipans, or ersatz marzipans, a poor man's substitute for almond marzipan.[15] Like many substitute foods, they acquired a character of their own over time and developed into something wholly new and different.

After the 1870s, when mold carving in general began to decline in the United States, many bakery supply firms, such as George Endriss of Philadelphia, copied the old molds in pewter, an innovation unique to this country. Earlier, several foundries in New York began casting molds in iron.

Terrell and Ward of Fishkill Landing on the Hudson and Shear, Packard and Company of Albany both included a number of New Year's cake molds with their line of waffle irons. The iron molds had one disadvantage—they shattered easily when dropped or exposed to sudden changes of temperature.

The pewter molds were very popular with small bakeries and housewives, more so even than the old wooden ones because the cold metal made the process of stamping the dough less troublesome. Stamping was generally accomplished by laying the mold facedown on the dough and pressing it with a rolling pin to the desired thickness. The large, elaborate wooden molds were extremely difficult for inexperienced bakers to handle and were sometimes placed in small presses. A stiff, near-frozen sheet of dough was "printed" like cold butter. This technique was not used in domestic cookery.

One could argue that while the molds themselves were artistic productions, their stock patterns and their commercial nature raise the question as to whether they are in fact folk art, or even part of folk cookery. For those cakes made in the home, the connectedness, the social context is clear. But as we shall see in the following chapter, commercialization forces us to redefine what we mean by *folk*.

Square cake print based on Conger prototypes and advertised by James Y. Watkins in *The Confectioners' Journal*, January 1899. Courtesy of Pat Guthman.

American wood Springerle mold from the 1880s using several stock motifs.

FUNERAL BISCUIT

1702

YIELD: APPROXIMATELY 2 DOZEN 4-INCH BISCUITS.

7 cups double-sifted pastry flour
¾ pound cold, lightly salted butter,
chopped
½ cup superfine sugar
3 tablespoons powdered ginger

1 tablespoon caraway seeds
2 eggs
1 cup unsulfured molasses
½ cup milk

Rub the flour, butter, sugar, and ginger through a large sieve to form fine crumbs. Toast the caraway seeds lightly for 5 to 8 minutes in an oven preheated to 350°F, then coarsely break them in a mortar. Add the broken seeds to the crumbs. Make a well in the center of the crumb mixture. Beat the eggs to a froth, add the molasses and milk, beat again, then pour this into the well. Using a large wooden fork or paddle, gently work the ingredients into a dough. *Do not knead.* Ripen the dough overnight in the refrigerator and keep the dough cold while working with it.

Preheat the oven to 375°F.

Roll the dough to a thickness of ¼–½ inch and stamp with a funeral-biscuit print. Lacking that, use a 2-inch or 4-inch butter mold; or simply cut the biscuits out with a tin cutter and prick patterns into the surface with a fork. Cut out the stamped biscuits and lay them on un-

greased baking sheets. Bake in the preheated oven for 10 to 15 minutes, or until the bottoms are golden brown.

NOTE:

This is called *short gingerbread* in the original manuscript recipe; it is actually a form of shortbread. Handling the dough too much will toughen the biscuits. These are best eaten with ale or beer.

SOURCE: Samuel Nutt, "Savorall Rare Sacrets and Choyce Curiossityes," Unpublished Memorandum Book. (Chester County, Pennsylvania, 1702–37), 57. Collection of the Chester County Historical Society, West Chester, Pennsylvania.

OPPOSITE PAGE: Butter prints from the nineteenth century. The left-hand print, from Ohio, was used as a cookie stamp and is stained from contact with molasses and gingerbread dough. The right-hand print is parched and worn from the repeated washings associated with stamping butter.

ELECTION CAKE

1874

*T*he Household, a popular monthly published in Brattleboro, Vermont, in the late nineteenth century, featured an active letter exchange among its subscribers. When a call went out for an authentic recipe for election cake, many readers responded. This recipe came from Boston. It is the plainest and one of the oldest election cake recipes in print. The method of preparation, the slow baking, and especially the combination of cassia and clove are all features of seventeenth-century American cookery. YIELD: ONE 10-INCH CAKE.

⅓ cup yellow cornmeal
1 cup cold water
8 tablespoons (1 stick) lightly salted butter
1 cup dark brown sugar
¼ ounce yeast proofed in 1 cup warm water sweetened with 1 tablespoon molasses

3 cups sifted all-purpose flour
1½ teaspoons powdered cassia (see note)
¼ teaspoon powdered clove

*B*eat together the cornmeal and water. Bring to a boil and scald the meal. Add the butter and sugar and beat over medium heat until the sugar is dissolved and the butter is melted. Set aside to cool. When lukewarm, add the proofed yeast, the flour, and the spices. If you prefer the cake very spicy, double the quantity of cassia and clove. In any case, at this stage, you should have a thick, stiffish batter.

Cover and set aside in a warm place to rise. When double in bulk (and covered with bubbles on the surface), pour the batter into a well-greased, 10-inch cake pan. Let the batter recover for 30 to 40 minutes, or until it rises to within half an inch of the top of the pan.

Preheat the oven to 350°F. After setting the cake in the middle of the oven, reduce heat to 300°F and bake for approximately 55 minutes. The cake is done when it tests dry in the center. Cool on a rack for a few minutes before removing from the pan. The crust will soften as the cake cools.

NOTE:

Election cake was originally baked in round loaves like bread. It was never iced, but it was sometimes glazed with egg yolk and molasses. Baking was done in broad earthenware dishes that are now difficult to procure. A 10-inch springform cake pan that is about 3 inches deep will suit this recipe perfectly.

For those unfamiliar with cassia, it is a spice—once very popular—that is similar in flavor to cinnamon but much more pungent. It is used a great deal in processing commercial chocolate and is the primary flavor in the little candy hearts known as "red hots." Cassia buds look somewhat like cloves and are frequently used like cloves in pickling. Cassia is usually available from shops specializing in herbs and spices.

SOURCE: *The Household* 8:11 (November 1874), 255.

NEW YEAR'S CAKE

1834

YIELD: APPROXIMATELY 3–4 DOZEN, DEPENDING
ON SIZE.

*½ pound (2 sticks) lightly
salted butter
2 cups sugar
1 cup sour cream*

*2 tablespoons caraway seeds
5 cups pastry flour
1 teaspoon baking soda
1½ teaspoons cream of tartar*

Cream the butter and sugar until light. Beat in the sour cream. Add the caraway seeds. Sift the flour, soda, and cream of tartar together twice, then sift dry mixture into the batter and work it up into a dough. Ripen the dough in the refrigerator 1 to 2 days before using.

Break off pieces of the dough and roll to a thickness of ½ inch. Press your wooden mold into the dough until it is no thinner than ¼-inch thick. Cut out the cookies with a sharp knife and rework the dough trimmings into the unused batch. Continue until all of the dough is used. Set the cookies on greased baking sheets no less than ¾ of an inch apart, and put the filled cookie sheets in a cool place overnight. This will dry the surface of the "pictures" so that they will not crack during baking. The next day, preheat the oven to 375°F. Bake the cookies for 10 to 12 minutes, or until pale golden on the bottom.

NOTE:

New Year's cake molds are now very rare, and the large ones cost many thousands of dollars on the antique market. Any cookie stamp or butter print can be used instead. Excellent and reasonably priced reproductions of New Year's cake and gingerbread molds are sold by Swiss Traditional Foods, Box 519, Milford, Pennsylvania 18337. An illustrated price list is available on request.

SOURCE: Phebe W. Underhill. "Receipt Book." (Long Island, New York, ca. 1834–1850). Roughwood Collection.

Conger rolling pin for New Year's Cake.

PAGES 122–123: **Conger New Year's Cake print. Courtesy of Chandler Saint.**

Compare this cake print with the Conger cake print
on pages 122–123. Note the use of stock motifs.
Courtesy of the Henry Francis du Pont
Winterthur Museum.

TRAINING CAKE

1874

YIELD: APPROXIMATELY 2 DOZEN COOKIES.

3 tablespoons lard or unsalted butter
2 tablespoons water
½ cup unsulfured molasses, or
¼ cup unsulfured molasses and
¼ cup honey

2 cups pastry flour
1 teaspoon baking soda
½ teaspoon salt
1½ teaspoons powdered ginger

Melt the butter with the water and add the molasses. Remove from the heat and beat to combine thoroughly. Sift the flour, soda, salt, and ginger together twice, then mix with the molasses and work up into a soft dough. If necessary, dust with additional flour to keep dough from becoming sticky. Cover and set in the refrigerator to ripen at least 2 hours or overnight.

Preheat the oven to 375°F.

Roll out the dough to a thickness of ¼ inch and cut into 2-inch round cookies. Prick each one with a fork to make decorative patterns on the surface. (This will keep the dough from blistering while it bakes.) Set the cookies on greased baking sheets and bake for 10 minutes.

SOURCE: *The Household* 7:3 (March 1874), 62.

From left to right: **Training Cake** (foreground); **Worcester Loaf** (as baked in a Turk's cap mold); **Worcester Loaf** baked in a pie dish and glazed with molasses; and **Salem Fancy Cake.**

SALEM FANCY CAKE
1833

This is a training-cake recipe from Salem, Massachusetts, that gained wide circulation in the 1820s and 1830s. The dough is quite soft and must be kept cold while it is being rolled. Unlike the molasses training cakes, which were usually stamped with designs, Salem fancy cake was left unornamented. Its richness needed no garnish.

YIELD: 3 DOZEN 2½-INCH COOKIES.

8 tablespoons (1 stick) lightly salted butter
2 tablespoons lard or Crisco
1 cup sugar

3 eggs
3 cups pastry flour
¾ teaspoon baking soda
1 tablespoon grated nutmeg

Cream the butter, lard, and sugar. Beat the eggs to a froth and combine with the butter mixture. Sift the flour, soda, and nutmeg together twice, then gradually sift dry mixture into the batter. Work this up into a soft dough, cover, and let stand in the refrigerator for 1 hour or until the dough is thoroughly cold. Preheat the oven to 350°F. Roll out dough to a thickness of ½ inch and cut into 2½-inch cookies. Set them on greased baking sheets and bake in the preheated oven for approximately 15 minutes.

SOURCE: *Lancaster Journal* (Lancaster, Pa.), January 17, 1833.

WORCESTER LOAF
1854

This is a classic example of the eighteenth-century American concept of cake: a species of rich bread that was the only dessert food many people ever tasted. It was served both as an election cake and as a funeral cake. For the diet-conscious of today, the plus is that Worcester loaf is not sugary sweet. The reason for this is that it was meant to be sliced and eaten with jam or preserves. Because it was used like bread, it was not iced. Best of all, it makes fabulous toast.

YIELD: AT LEAST ONE 10-INCH CAKE.

1 tablespoon sugar
¼ ounce yeast
1 cup lukewarm water
8 tablespoons (1 stick) unsalted butter
2 cups milk
6 cups all-purpose flour
¼ cup sugar
3 eggs

Dissolve the sugar and yeast in the water and proof. Melt the butter in the milk by warming it over a low heat. Sift the flour and sugar into a mixing bowl and form a well in the middle. Beat the eggs to a froth and combine with the yeast. When the milk-and-butter mixture is tepid, combine with the eggs and yeast and pour this into the well. Work the ingredients into a thick batter and pour it into a greased turk's-cap or Bundt mold. Cover and let rise until the batter is level with the rim of the cake pan, about 2 to 3 hours. Bake in an oven preheated to 350°F for 45 to 50 minutes. Cool on a rack before turning out of the mold. Best served the next day.

OPPOSITE PAGE: Redware cake pan made by molding clay over a copper cake pan. In this case, the folk potter has borrowed his design directly from a nonfolk form.

NOTE:

The batter in this recipe is extremely active and likely to overflow in warm weather. If your cake mold is 4½ inches deep and 10 inches in diameter (the most common size), it will probably be too small. Since larger molds are hard to come by, I suggest reserving 2 cups of batter and baking them separately in a small cake pan.

I prefer to bake Worcester loaf another way: in greased shallow pie plates, letting it rise up into small round loaves. These are quite handsome when glazed in the old style with a mixture of dark molasses and water (1 tablespoon molasses to 1½ tablespoons water). When baking is done—for small loaves 35 minutes at 350°F should be sufficient—remove them from the oven, brush them with the glaze, and return to the oven for 5 minutes to allow the glaze to set. The finish should shine like shellac.

SOURCE: *Agricultural Almanac for 1855* (Lancaster, Pa., 1854).

Children picking potatoes, Montgomery County, Pennsylvania.
Photograph by H. Winslow Fegley, circa 1890.
Courtesy of the Schwenkfelder Library.

The Industrial Revolution did not come quickly to all parts of the country. The 1840s and 1850s saw huge technological changes in the way food was produced and the way in which kitchen equipment was redesigned for a mass market. The Civil War determined the outcome of this process in favor of the industrial North, but folk patterns remained intact in many of the former culture hearths, and they served as colorful material in American prints—like those of Currier and Ives—and in high art, like William Sidney Mount's *Eel-Spearing at Setauket*. In fact, the very popularity of these American themes was itself evidence of a growing nostalgia about an America that existed in a more idyllic past.

Even in 1900, one did not need to travel far from Philadelphia to find Pennsylvania Dutch children digging *Grumbiere* (potatoes) to carry home in old splint baskets. And one did not need to travel far from Pittsburgh to find "snake" fences or Cohees eating ramps, or go too far east of Akron, Ohio, to find vestiges of colonial Connecticut transplanted there after the Revolution.

In the South, post–Civil War poverty prolonged culinary patterns established in the seventeenth century. Henry Glassie, for example, mentioned interviews with Virginia informants in the 1960s who told how songbirds, especially chickadees, robins, and blackbirds, were made into pies filled with white gravy.[1] Songbird pies were once an esteemed folk dish in early America. The blackbird, in particular, because it fed on wild rice, was viewed as a succulent delicacy equal to English snipe.[2] *Warner's Safe Cook Book* (Rochester, N.Y., 1891) included several old up-country recipes for blackbird, among them the once popular snack, blackbird on toast.[3]

Even when massive immigration brought an influx of new peoples into the old culture hearths, they were forced to adjust their cultures to the preexisting models—one of the axioms of human migration. The many minority diets that came to exist side by side with established

American patterns found a native cookery that was strange, moving quickly out of its agricultural context and into something new, unfamiliar, and by and large distrusted. Many Americans, like Harriet Beecher Stowe, viewed it not as a cookery "on the move" but as a cookery on the decline.[4]

More than any other single force, the cookstove brought a radical change to the art of cookery. The rules that applied in the past, the techniques and oral traditions that had been relied on for centuries, were suddenly obsolete. American folk cookery was set adrift for awhile until cooks became accustomed to this very peculiar and

demanding invention. It became less a matter of creative continuity than one of massive readjustment. It was as if the cooks had been forced to learn a new food dialect.

Songs of Saleratus

It started with saleratus, or more correctly, with its immediate predecessor, pearl ash, the panacea of all baking woes. This wonder baking powder came into American folk cookery through New York.

Prior to the general introduction of pearl ash in the 1820s, folk cooks leavened their breadstuffs with homemade yeast, or more rarely with eggs (the most expensive way), or by beating the dough to break it down into microscopic layers of fiber, as in beaten biscuits. Beating the dough made the biscuits soft and flaky.

The Dutch bakers who settled in colonial New Netherlands were familiar with another method of leavening their baked goods: the use of alkaline powders. This was a technique known among professional bakers in Europe since the Middle Ages, and trade in these powders was considerable. The Europeans made a substance called pearl ash from refined wood ash or from the refined ash of a Spanish seaweed called *barilla.* They also used refined salts from the ash of deer antlers called *Hirschhornsalz,* which is still used in Germany instead of baking powder.

In colonial New York, where wood was cheap, potash became a major export product in the eighteenth century. The New York method for making potash was much discussed at the time, and a description of the process was published in 1788 in the *Pennsylvania Gazette.*[5]

In order to make potash, one needed to begin with lye, and this required an *ash gum,* an implement that was once common

Ash gum, circa 1745–1750. Hewn from a single log (now cracked), the gum was placed on a bench to drain. A stone in the bottom regulated the flow of lye.

OPPOSITE PAGE: The "American Cooking Stove" by Shear, Packard & Company, Albany, New York. Note the bulge pot at the back of the stove. Wood engraving from an advertising brochure, 1869. (Roughwood Collection)

in most rural American households. The term *gum* is an old dialect word for anything made from a hollowed-out log, as in *gum crib,* a cradle made from a hollowed-out log, and *bee-gum,* a beehive made from a hollow log.

Wood ashes were sifted and placed in the gum, and water was then poured over them. The alkaline drainings or lye were collected in tubs and then boiled in large kettles until reduced to a salt or powder. This powder was further refined by subjecting it to intense heat which melted it. This purified potash was usually white or "pearly" in color—hence the name pearl ash—and more concentrated than potash in its chemical activity.

New York housewives used pearl ash in cookery. It was a necessary leavening agent in New Year's cakes, and it was used to make a once well known semisweet cracker called New York potash cake.

Potassium bicarbonate, or saleratus, from the Latin *sal-aeratus* (literally "aerated salt"), was a commercial improvement over pearl ash. By the 1840s it was being marketed in many parts of the country under a variety of patented names. As might be expected, the chemical activity of these saleratuses varied with the additives and patented compounds mixed with them, but they were all sold in basically the same manner. They came in paper envelopes with recipes enclosed or printed on the outside. From these recipes it is evident that saleratus was somewhat stronger in its chemical activity than the baking soda of today. To achieve similar results, it is usually necessary to use 1¼ teaspoons of baking soda for every teaspoon of saleratus called for in old recipes.

Saleratus changed the nature of American folk cookery. It allowed poor women to bake bread without yeast. It made possible the dry, crumbly corn breads that we know today—impossible to make with pearl ash, since it gave cornmeal, as a period cook once remarked, a "vile flavor." Saleratus made it possible to reduce the number of eggs in cake recipes and therefore lower their cost and preparation time. And when American iron foundries began selling cookstoves, the instruction sheets for using them usually included complimentary recipes showing the happy owner how to make hitherto undreamed of dessert pastries with saleratus. Saleratus worked remarkably well in cast-iron cookstoves because it required a "fast" or "soaking" heat. Iron cookstoves—before the days of oven thermometers—baked fast, and the folk cook was thus required to shift from old-style slow baking techniques to the new quick ones.

The intense heat of the cookstove proved destructive to the redware that

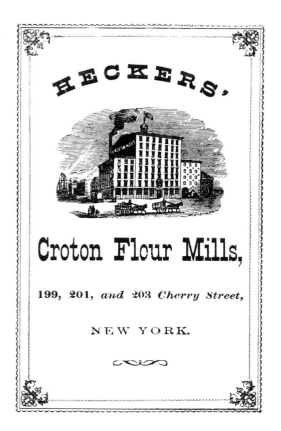

HECKERS'
FARINA JELLY MOLDS
Of Various Sizes, Forms, and Patterns,

From one gill to two quarts in capacity,

SUCH AS

Clusters of Roses.	**Ears of Corn.**
Turkish Turban.	**Pine-Apple.**
Clusters of Fruit.	**Lion's Face and Mane.**
Grecian Rose and Cactus	**Etc., etc., etc.**

These molds are now for sale at the principal stores that furnish housekeeping articles, or can be obtained at the Croton Mills.

Promotional cookbook from 1869 with an advertisement for yellowware jelly molds. (Roughwood Collection)

most country cooks used in cooking and baking. This low-fired earthenware often cracked or exploded under the intense heat of the narrow, cramped ovens in cookstoves. Commercial potteries took advantage of this in the 1830s and 1840s by introducing cheap, mass-produced yellowware that was fired at a higher temperature and had a clay body more resistant to cookstove heat. East Liverpool, Ohio, and northern New Jersey—particularly South Amboy—became centers of yellowware production, but potteries sprang up in many other places as well.[6] Some of the potteries copied old traditional forms, but in general, standardization changed the shape of traditional dishes. The quail pot pie recipe at the end of this chapter, for example, called specifically for a yellowware baking dish.

Likewise, as roller mills in the East began to produce newer and more finely ground flours in the 1850s and 1860s, and particularly with the introduction of commercial cornstarch, farina, cornstarch, and flour puddings became extremely popular. They were substitute foods for the elegant almond blancmanges of upper-class cookery in the eighteenth and early nineteenth centuries. Many firms, like Hecker's Croton Flour Mills in New York, sold commercial pudding molds to be used with these recipes.[7]

Yellowware and ironstone Boston cups
in a variety of glazes.

The commercialization of pottery wares did not entirely break down regionalization. In New England, for example, *Boston cups* achieved local popularity, as Maria Parloa described in 1887:

These stone cups will last twenty years or more, and be perfectly sweet at the end of that time. Brown or yellow earthenware, or even stone-china cups, will absorb fat, and soon acquire a strong and disagreeable odor and flavor; besides, they break and crack easily. Outside of New England these stone cups sometimes are called Boston cups— probably because they are used so generally in New England, and Boston is the chief place of distribution.[8]

Boston cups were used for baking puffs or popovers, foods that were easy to make in the intense heat of the iron cookstove.

The foundries that produced cookstoves also cast equipment for use with them. In some cases, like cast-iron brown-bread pans, the *hollow ware* (as cast-iron cookware was called) mimicked traditional forms; usually, however, it did not. The Griswold foundry in Erie, Pennsylvania, for example, sold a square frying pan that was introduced in 1865. Nathaniel Waterman, a house-furnishings merchant in Boston, took out patents in 1859 on a large assortment of cast-iron muffin pans, several of which drew their forms directly from older redware.[9] Waterman's "Wisconsin cake pans" were extremely popular from 1860 to 1890 for making cornmeal "gems," as quick muffins were called. The term *gem* came from the name of a commercial baking powder used to leaven the muffins.

The original Wisconsin cake, however, was hardly gemlike. It was a coarse wheat-bran muffin introduced by abolitionist cooks to avoid having to use ingredients produced by slave labor. As the country became more and more polarized by the slavery issue before the Civil War, these boycott recipes, like honey tea cake (no slave molasses), found their way into the folk repertoire, but not always with happy results, as this account from Ohio relates:

So intense was the feeling against slavery, that many became strongly opposed to using anything which had been produced by slave labor, and while some went only to a certain extent, others took advantage of the opportunity offered and went so far as to discard tea and coffee and restrict themselves to the use of Graham bread, made in the simplest manner. The change from the more luxurious mode of living was so great that it operated with fatal result in some instances, and one whole family in the neighborhood of Wilmington was nearly blotted out because of its adherence to the new regime.[10]

OPPOSITE PAGE: **Advertisement for Warner's Safe Yeast from 1887. (Roughwood Collection)**

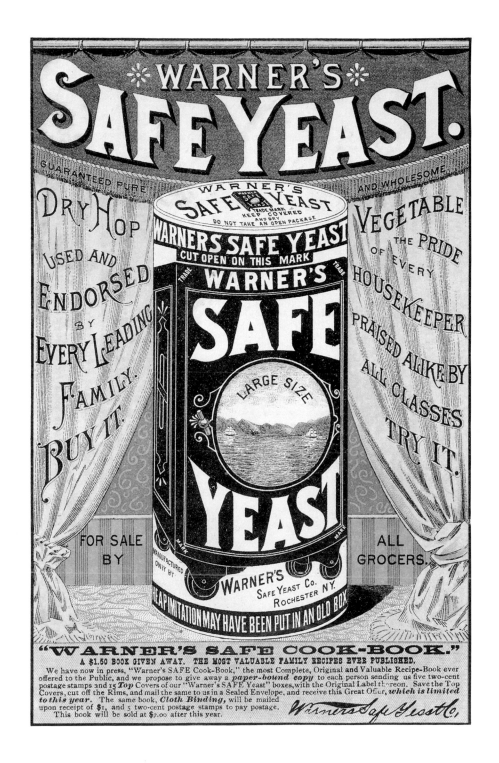

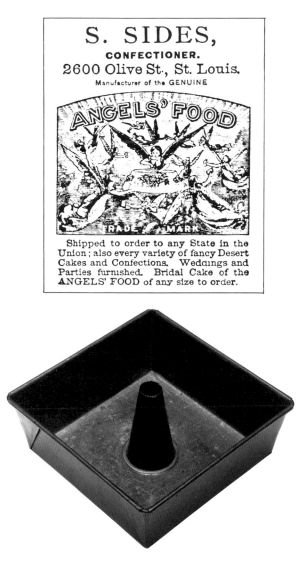

S. SIDES,
CONFECTIONER.
2600 Olive St., St. Louis.
Manufacturer of the GENUINE

ANGELS' FOOD

TRADE MARK

Shipped to order to any State in the Union; also every variety of fancy Desert Cakes and Confections. Weddings and Parties furnished. Bridal Cake of the ANGELS' FOOD of any size to order.

TOP: From *The Confectioners' Journal*, November 1878

BOTTOM: Original angel food cake pan

OPPOSITE PAGE: From the Boston city directory for 1859

I suspect that the "fatal result" was not due so much to malnutrition as it was to the remarkable strength of wheat-bran muffins, which Mrs. Rorer promoted in the 1890s because, to use her words, they "are exceedingly good for constipation."[11]

More pervasive even than radical abolitionist cookery was the effect of Temperance on the American folk diet. The zeal with which the Temperance movement stripped old foodways from American culture and retreaded them into "Christian cookery" is obvious in the cider-jelly recipe at the end of this chapter. But it is perhaps most eloquently demonstrated by the Non-Fermentation movement, a religiously inspired effort to turn Americans from the use of yeast, since yeast, even in bread, produces alcohol.

The *Good Cook's Hand Book*, which was distributed gratis in the 1860s and 1870s by agents for "Horsford's Self-Raising Bread Preparation," brought the thrust of this movement to the grass-roots level. Not only did this baking powder claim to prevent rickets, cholera, and tooth decay, it purportedly promoted muscle and bone growth, and unlike "other yeast," did not "decompose" flour or produce alcohol.[12] It made gas.

Patent-medicine companies, like H. H. Warner of Rochester, New York, which sold "Warner's Safe Cure" for kidney and

liver ailments, also produced a "Safe Yeast" that was a nonfermenting product. By sending in box tops from the chemical yeast—one had to use fifteen boxes of the large size—one would receive "the most valuable family recipes ever published": *Warner's Safe Cook Book.*

The word *family* is important here, because it was clearly understood to mean *country,* or what we today would call *folk,* or *down home.* The Warner cookbook is chock-full of real American folk recipes, from bonny-clabber and green pea fritters, to "shred" cod fish and blackbird pie. It is obvious that in directing its product advertising at rural Americans, Warner fully intended to win converts through the stomach.

The Non-Fermentation movement produced hundreds of food products centering on this theme. Angel food cake, invented by Linus T. Dexter of Vineland, New Jersey, was one that is still with us today.[13] Bickham and Huffman's "Cream Puff Baking Yeast" of the 1870s lingers on in the firm's trade name, which has now become a part of American speech.[14]

The Bulge Pot Comes of Age

While Temperance chipped away at the structure of American folk cookery, the invasion of the cookstove shifted the material culture of the kitchen away from the hearth and into new regions of creative design. American cast iron has long been ignored as an art form, but it is one of the high points of our inventiveness. The aesthetics of designs created somewhere else by a person unknown to the folk cook worked on two levels. Obviously, she was forced to make her recipes fit unfamiliar pots. But on the other hand, objects that met the demands of perfect use, objects that "fit" the human scale of her hands and kitchen, gave the cook greater expressive control over her art.

Mass-produced objects have always been found in American kitchens. In 1796, for example, Isaac Tomlinson of New Haven, Connecticut, advertised "freshly imported" hardware and dry goods, including brass kettles, sheet iron, and iron hollow ware.[15] The Carron Iron Foundry in Scotland dumped vast shipments of finished hollow ware on the colonial market, even while Americans were exporting high-grade pig iron.

Most eighteenth-century metal culinary equipment used in this country was produced in foreign workshops employing many hands, each assigned to finish a certain part of the design. Wrought-iron toasters, gridirons, and bird broilers, for example, were usually finished in this way. And if one studies enough old iron equipment, it is often possible to group individual pieces into lots by handle design or some other telling detail. It is not unusual to find identical pieces, which of course suggests a degree of mass production far more extensive than we have supposed. American craftsmen were for the most part supplemental to the market until after the Revolution. They did a large trade in repairs and recycling of broken equipment.

Federal Furnace, near Plymouth, Massachusetts, advertised in 1796 that it would gladly contract for "particular kinds of iron ware, shapes, etc." in small or large quantities.[16] Even hollow ware could be custom made. This opens an area of research that has never been undertaken, at least not thoroughly, and would probably produce quite startling insights into regionalisms in American cast iron. For the time, let the bulge pot serve as an example.

Bulge pot was the commercial term used by nineteenth-century foundries for the large, squat stewpots that were sold as accessories with iron cookstoves. The wood engraving of the "American cooking

OPPOSITE PAGE: *Cooking pots from left to right:* Huntington, Long Island, redware stewpot *(back left)*, circa 1815; Norwalk, Connecticut, brownware "baker" *(foreground)*, circa 1830—lacks lid; Norwalk, Connecticut, redware stewpot *(center)*, circa 1825—lacks lid; Albany, New York, iron *bulge pot*, circa 1849; Pennsylvania German redware cookpot with iron pot pusher, circa 1865–1880.

Samp or suppan

Stewed Apples, Onions,
and Potatoes with
Wholemeal Dumplings.
See recipe on page 146.

Stewed Ground Cherries
with Chives and Coriander,
a typical Pennsylvania Dutch
summer dish

"Stew Pot No. 3" (lid missing) by John Safford, Monmouth, Maine, circa 1850. Courtesy of Old Sturbridge Village.

stove" in this chapter shows a bulge pot resting on the back griddle directly behind a water kettle. Its flared rim is designed to hold a close-fitting tin lid. Commercial bulge pots were usually numbered to indicate size, and that same number also appeared on the lid, unless it happened to be a replacement of later manufacture.

In the Middle States, earthenware bulge pots predated the iron ones by at least eighty years, perhaps even more. Redware bulge-pot production centered in Connecticut, particularly in the area of Norwalk. On Long Island, there were potteries in the vicinity of Huntington. And there were many active potteries in northern New Jersey that made bulge pots of a very localized design. The bulge pot appears to be an entirely unique American development in that there are no direct antecedents in English redware pottery. It is a classic example of the kind of creative process that occurred in the early culture hearths along the Atlantic Seaboard.

The users of bulge pots—the folk cooks —generally called them *stewpots*. There are probably other names that have now been lost, but *stewpot* seems to be the most common term, and that is the word also used by the Safford Pottery in Monmouth, Maine. The Saffords produced their own version of the bulge pot between 1840 and 1870 and sometimes stamped the pots with the words *Stew Pot*.[17] A very fine example of this, marked *Stew Pot No. 3,* is now in the collection of Old Sturbridge Village in Massachusetts. The Safford pots, which came with lids, bear a resemblance to the old tall cookpots used by the Pennsylvania Germans and discussed in chapter 1. Both may have evolved out of a shared medieval tradition.

The earthenware stewpots came in many sizes, from the one- or two-gallon Long Island pots used for samp (a grade of hominy similar in texture to rice), to the small one-quart "bakers" made in brownware by the pottery of Absolom Day (1770–1843) in Norwalk, Connecticut.[18] The popularity of the brownware bakers is evident in the fact that considerable advice has survived on their use and care. The following is from the Methodist *Christian Advocate and Journal* of June 21, 1839:

> It is a good plan to put new earthenware into cold water, and let it heat gradually until it boils, then cool again. Brown earthenware, in particular, may be toughened in this way. A handful of rye or wheat bran thrown in while it is boiling, will preserve the glazing, so that it will not be destroyed by acid or salt.

The method of cooking in stewpots or bakers was quite simple. They were filled with ingredients, the lid was put tightly in

Redware stewpot with original lid. Courtesy of Old Sturbridge Village.

place, and then they were set down in the hot hearth ashes to simmer. Or, they were set on a trivet inside a cast-iron "boiler"— a large pot or kettle for boiling meat. Hot water was then brought up to the neck, and as the water boiled gently, the contents steam-baked. Tough fowl were sometimes cooked this way. In general, these vessels were used for meals like the one described in *The Household* in 1874:

> A delicious little stew can be made of about equal parts onion, potato and apple. Peel and quarter three onions, and put them to stew in double their measure of water for forty-five minutes (for red or yellow onions one hour). Then cut up and add three medium-sized potatoes, and three apples, pared, quartered and cored. Then, upon one gill of wheat meal, pour boiling water enough to scald it, stirring it lightly; and when the stew boils up, after putting in the potatoes and apples, add this dough, in bits as big as an almond, and not compact. Cover close and stew gently until the potatoes are done.[19]

Stewpots were used not just for cooking but for storing fat for the griddle, as containers for homemade yeast, and even as cookie jars. Those pots used for cookery that have survived over the years are generally charred on the bottom, heavily scratched about the belly, and usually lack their lids. Escaping steam often rattled the ceramic lids and caused them to crack or break, the only design flaw in these pots.

When domestic cookery shifted to the cookstove, the earthenware stewpot could not withstand the intense heat; thus it was necessary to translate this utensil into cast iron. The iron bulge pot evolved in New England but was quickly imitated elsewhere. It was valued far more highly by cooks than its earthenware ancestor because the surface of the iron became smooth with use. Thus, the pots increased in value, unlike the earthenware ones, and realized better prices at country sales. As Maria Parloa put it in 1887: "If a housekeeper can have but one kind of pan, it will be wise to have the cast-iron kind."[20]

A "comic" calendar from the 1880s shows a black family seated around the Thanksgiving table. The eldest son, returning from college, is just entering the door. Not only has a New England custom gone South and crossed the racial boundary, but there, on the corner of the table, soiling the linen, is a bulge pot full of stew. In a sense, this cartoon captures the deeper currents of change and continuity that characterized American folk culture at the time. But it is an image of a folk culture whose connectedness is no longer with the land but with the factory, the union hall, and now, the shopping center and outlet. It is the beginning of a different kind of "folk."

Iron bulge pot on the Thanksgiving table of a
Southern black family. From a comic advertising
calendar, New York, circa 1882.
(Roughwood Collection)

NEW YORK POTASH CAKE
1821

YIELD: APPROXIMATELY 3–4 DOZEN BISCUITS.

1 cup milk
½ cup sugar
4 cups pastry flour (see note)

½ teaspoon baking soda
8 tablespoons (1 stick) cold, unsalted butter

Scald the milk and dissolve the sugar in it. Set aside to cool. Sift 3½ cups of the flour with the baking soda three times to mix them thoroughly. Chop the butter into pea-sized pieces and, using a sieve, work it to a fine crumb with the sifted flour. Make a well in the center and add the sweetened milk. Work this into a soft dough and add only enough additional flour for the dough to be kneaded like bread. Knead vigorously at least 10 minutes, or until the dough is spongy and pliant.

Preheat the oven to 425°F.

Roll out dough to a thickness of ¼ inch and cut into 2-inch rounds. Prick each biscuit with a fork and bake on greased cookie sheets for approximately 10 to 13 minutes, or until golden brown on the bottom.

NOTE:

These are similar in texture to English milk biscuits. They cannot be made with all-purpose flour.

SOURCE: Dr. Thomas Cooper, ed. *The Domestic Encyclopedia.* (Philadelphia: Abraham Small, 1821), vol. 3, 133.

WISCONSIN CAKES
1865

Wisconsin cakes were made in cast-iron "gem" pans. The Truman & Shaw household catalogue, a kind of Williams Sonoma catalogue of the 1860s, makes particular reference to "these peculiar shaped pans," which at the time were quite a novelty. They were invented, or at least patented, by Nathaniel Waterman of Boston in 1859. YIELD: 2 DOZEN MUFFINS.

1 cup whole wheat (Graham) flour
½ cup white flour
1 teaspoon baking powder
½ teaspoon salt

2 eggs, separated
1 cup milk
2 tablespoons maple syrup

Sift the whole wheat flour, white flour, baking powder, and salt. Beat the egg yolks and combine with the milk and maple syrup. Mix the wet and dry ingredients. Beat the egg whites until stiff, then fold them into the batter.

Preheat the oven to 360°F, and if you are using a cast-iron muffin pan, set it in the oven until it is hot (about 5 minutes). Remove from the oven and grease each of the cups in the pan. Then pour enough batter in each cup to fill it two-thirds full—Waterman pans take about 1½ tablespoons of batter per cup. Return the pan to the oven and bake 20 minutes.

NOTE:

If you have two muffin pans, I would recommend baking the two batches together, since the batter loses air the longer it stands. Muffins baked in tin will not puff as nicely as those baked in iron.

SOURCE: Truman & Shaw. *Catalogue of Housekeepers, Builders, and Miscellaneous Hardware and Tools.* (Phila.: Kildare, Printer, 1865), 6.

HONEY TEA CAKE

Before 1834

This is the old and once well known recipe of Elizabeth Margaret Chandler (1807–34), an abolitionist poet who settled in Tecumseh, Michigan, in 1830. Her fiery poems were published by another well-known abolitionist, Benjamin Lundy. Her honey cake was the toast of abolitionist teas because it did not use molasses, a product of slave labor.

YIELD: ONE 2 x 10 x 10-INCH CAKE.

8 tablespoons (1 stick) unsalted butter, at room temperature
1 cup honey
½ cup sour cream

2 eggs
2 cups pastry flour
½ teaspoon baking soda
1 tablespoon cream of tartar

Preheat the oven to 350°F.

Cream the butter and honey together until smooth. Add the sour cream and beat well. Beat the eggs to a froth and combine with the batter. Sift the flour, baking soda, and cream of tartar together three times (to ensure a light cake), then sift this into the batter. Stir well, but do not beat too hard, or the soda will be overactivated before baking. Pour into a well-greased 10-inch square pan and bake for 30 minutes.

NOTE:

A 10-inch round cake pan may be used for this recipe. The term *tea cake* meant that it was baked round and cut into eighths. This cake also takes well to elaborately shaped molds.

SOURCE: Dr. C. C. Miller. *Food Value of Honey. Honey Cooking Recipes.* (Medina, Ohio: A. I. Root Co., ca. 1910), 12.

OPPOSITE PAGE: **Many early commercial pans were adapted from older folk models.** *From left to right:* **Honey Tea Cakes baked in a Waterman muffin pan; an iron brown bread pan derived from the deep patty-pan form (compare it with the small redware cup beside it); an oval redware baking cup; and on the bottom right, Wisconsin cakes baked in a Waterman pan with similar oval cups.**

CIDER JELLY
1891

Many Victorian molded jellies, especially those intended for Christmas, contained rum or wine. A Lutheran version of this recipe, from Canajoharie, New York, added brandy to the cider, but not enough to make it noticeably alcoholic.[21] Since this was a Temperance recipe issued for a Methodist Christmas bazaar in 1891, fresh cider was the required choice of the cook.

YIELD: APPROXIMATELY 6 SERVINGS.

5 envelopes unflavored gelatin
(see note)
2 cups sugar
Grated zest of 1 lemon
¼ teaspoon powdered cinnamon or
4 drops oil of cassia (see note)

1 cup cold water
Juice of 2 lemons
1 quart sweet cider

Mix the gelatin, sugar, lemon zest, and cinnamon. Pour the cold water over this and stir to dissolve the sugar. Then add the lemon juice. Bring the cider to a boil. If scum rises, skim it off; then pour the cider over the gelatin mixture. Stir until the gelatin is completely dissolved, then set aside to cool. When cool, but not set, pour into a cold 1-quart mold and let stand in the refrigerator until stiff. Unmold and serve.

NOTE:

When using a mold, it is always necessary to increase the amount of gelatin so that it will be stiff enough to stand. If you are not using a mold or do not intend to turn the jelly out of a bowl, then the gelatin can be reduced to 3 envelopes. Also, if you wish to use oil of cassia, which is far superior in this recipe to cinnamon, add the oil after the gelatin has begun to cool; otherwise it will evaporate.

SOURCE: Esopus Methodist Episcopal Church. *The Cook's Manual and Buyer's Director.* (Rondout, N.Y.: Kingston Freeman, 1891), 42.

OPPOSITE PAGE: **Cider Jelly and various yellowware jelly molds, 1850–1870**

QUAIL POT PIE

1917

This is a recipe from the old Palmer House Hotel in Chicago, which was well known for its midwestern game cookery. The nice thing about this recipe is its flexibility. The original calls for six wild squab, but as passenger pigeons are now extinct, quail makes an acceptable substitute. My temptation is to suggest squirrel, which is the game meat par excellence of American folk cookery (two small squirrels may be used in this recipe), but my publisher is not enthusiastic. I admit that there is a world of difference between the frolicking creatures in Central Park and the acorn-fed squirrels from the back hills of North Carolina or Tennessee. And after all, no one has gotten the bright idea yet to raise squirrel commercially, even though in flavor it is far superior to rabbit. YIELD: 6 TO 8 SERVINGS.

2 tablespoons unsalted butter
⅓ cup diced salt pork
6 quail, cut into quarters
3 tablespoons all-purpose flour
1 cup minced onion
2½ cups hot water

4 potatoes, sliced
1 teaspoon salt
¼ teaspoon white pepper
½ teaspoon powdered mace
12 dumplings (see note)
1 short crust

Melt the butter in a deep stewing pan and fry the salt pork. When it begins to brown, dust the quail with the flour and fry it on both sides until light brown. Then add the onion. When the onion is wilted, add the water and bring to a boil.

Preheat the oven to 350°F.

Cut the sliced potatoes into squares about the size of postage stamps, then make layers of potato and fried quail in a deep, 2-quart baking dish. Season with salt, pepper, and mace. Pour the liquid from the stewing pan over this and cover the top with dumplings. Lay the crust over this, crimp and ornament with pastry figures, and cut two or three vents to let steam escape. Bake the pie in the oven for 45 to 55 minutes, or until the potatoes are cooked.

In the nineteenth century, pot-pie dumplings were usually made with flour and mutton fat or beef suet. With the advent of baking-powder cookery after the Civil War, soft, fluffy dumplings came into fashion—promoted by the baking-powder manufacturers as healthier.

POT PIE DUMPLINGS

The Palmer House recipe does not clarify the sort of dumplings intended, but I suspect they were like the dumpling recipe I have appended below. Another combination that is well worth trying is the corn drop dumpling recipe on page 24. Cook the corn drop dumplings separately as directed, rather than in the pie, and serve with the pie when it is taken to the table. YIELD: 12 DUMPLINGS.

Yolks of 2 hard-boiled eggs
2 teaspoons unsalted butter, softened
1 egg white

2 tablespoons all-purpose flour
Salt and pepper

Grate the egg yolks and work to a paste with the butter. Beat the egg white until stiff, then add to the paste with the flour and seasonings. Dust your work surface with flour and form the paste into marble-size balls. Set these in the pot pie as directed.

SOURCE: *The Capitol Cook Book.* (Akron, Ohio: The Saalfield Publishing Co., 1917), 87.

Trade card, Boston, circa 1880. (Roughwood Collection)

Coming Up Cans

Sometime in the latter part of the nineteenth century, American folk cookery began to define itself in terms of the tin can: what came in cans, what one learned from cans, what one could do with cans after they were used. Whole dinners could be conjured from cans. Even meat came in cans. Large hominy rarely came any other way.

Some cans contained foods that older cooks remembered from Grandmother's day, like elderberries, which were once a staple of the folk diet—the dried ones took the place of raisins. Other cans were decorated with Revolutionary War heroes or Indians, and this suggested a connection, in the distant past, with the log cabin in which everyone's ancestor had lived.

The ladies of New England built a log cabin at the American Centennial Exposition in 1876, and thousands of visitors from all walks of life saw it. They saw the spinning wheels, the rag carpets, the tall clock, and the bean vines running up the front. The beans, a patriotic plant, were necessary for Boston baked beans, a preparation like Boston brown bread that was also available in tins. There was a mysterious virtue, a sense of impending progress, once Americans discovered that they could put folk culture into a can. It meant opening up China with beef jerky. It meant

The New England Kitchen at the Centennial Exposition in Philadelphia, 1876. From a contemporary wood engraving.
(Roughwood Collection)

A nostalgic assortment of furnishings arranged for display in the kitchen of the Van Cortlandt house in New York, circa 1900. In the foreground, a James Y. Watkins New Year's cake print intended to emphasize the Dutch ancestry of the Van Cortlandts. At right, a similar print, circa 1900. Courtesy of Chandler Saint.

OPPOSITE PAGE: From *The Confectioners' Journal*, September 1875.

conquering Cuba with pumpkin pie. Everywhere in the world, America was coming up cans.

Then in 1884 came Lafcadio Hearn's *La Cuisine Creole,* and American cookery was riveted to attention. Suddenly we were reminded of our culinary roots, the ones we had neglected in our rush to the canneries. Lucia Swett, not satisfied with the manner in which history had passed by New England bread making, brought forth her *New England Breads, Luncheon and Tea Biscuits* in 1891, a genteel collection of proper Boston muffins and rolls.

In 1894 Sarah Tyson Rorer of Philadelphia Cooking School fame published her pocket-tome *Colonial Recipes,* which included a very unlikely recipe for Martha Washington's pumpkin pie, but one that was easy to make. Queen of the Republican Court, Martha became the rallying point for the women of America, the bluish lens through which our culinary past was to be seen. Patriotism was swelling, and the war with Spain proved that Margaret Hooker's *Υᵉ Gentlewoman's Housewifery* (New York, 1896) had appeared none too soon, for it gave us the *authentick* story.

There followed a spate of nostalgia books, many of them from the pen of Alice Morse Earle. The mythology of early America was thus thickened up, given shape and form. It was a skimming-off pro-

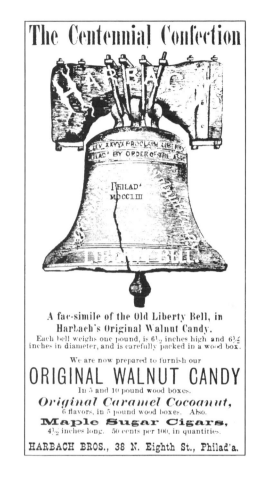

cess that whisked the cream of the Republican Court but left the buttermilk pressings of folk culture to run off in the clay.

Yet things were happening that even the Alice Earles quite overlooked. The Centennial introduced an enormous new range of foods, and for the first time, in the various national restaurants at the exhibition, Americans tasted strange dishes they had only read about. It was an opening up of taste. Centennial cake, brought out at the fair, went home to the back counties of Pennsylvania, where it became shoo-fly pie, a molasses crumb cake baked in a pie shell, which is now sold as an invention of the Pennsylvania Dutch. *Caveat emptor:* Without molasses, it is like vanilla ice cream without vanilla.

In the Midwest, we find prosperity cookies and Minnehaha cake, the latter named for the suicidal Indian princess whose waterfalls still mourn her death in a Minneapolis park. In Virginia, we find watermelon cake, with Southern deference to "darky" humor. In Massachusetts, we find D.A.R. pudding and a drop cookie called "Hannahette." In New Haven,

Connecticut, we find Mrs. Culver's peanut butter griddle cakes, a blend of something new (peanut butter) with that old New England pancake discussed earlier in this book.[1] And in Erie, Pennsylvania, the Griswold iron foundries unveiled their patent colonial breakfast skillet, subdivided into three compartments, one for the colonial bacon, one for the colonial hash browns, and one for the colonial egg, sunny-side up. In this unique skillet, an entire colonial meal was condensed and frozen for time in iron. It was America's first TV dinner, long before TV.

In Keene, New Hampshire, the Taft Pottery brought out a patent earthenware saucepan for use on the cookstove. Its design was a revival of the old colonial *pip-*

Colonial Revival pipkin by J. S. Taft,
Keene, New Hampshire, 1870.
Courtesy of Old Sturbridge Village.

Colonial breakfast skillet, Erie, Pennsylvania,
circa 1910.

kin, in this case, a pipkin without feet. In fact, cooking in stoneware grew so much in popularity by the end of the 1890s that it was even called a "renaissance," in spite of the prevalence of iron cookware at the time.[2] Actually, this "renaissance" was the result of the Arts and Crafts movement sifting down into the kitchens of working-class America.

In short, the creative process of American folk cookery did not halt with the attack of the cookstove and the invasion of tin cans. It continued in the reinvention of the old put to use in new ways. It was Scott's chowder, which alluded to the days when chowders were only seamen's fare.[3] It was trench stew and the patriotism of refighting the Revolution from a picnic basket at the Valley Forge Martha Washington Log Cabin Tea Room. It was Baltimore crab gumbo and the hopeful vision of blending the best of Lafcadio Hearn with Fort McHenry. It was maple sugar candy, not boiled in the shade of Vermont's Green Mountains but poured from a log-cabin-shaped bottle, mixed with sugar, and served with a rubber of bridge long before the maple leaves were down. It was Higdom, a new look for an old hash that could raise money for the parsonage roof. And it

OPPOSITE PAGE: **Colonial Revival pie plate by Simon Singer, Bucks County, Pennsylvania, 1886. Made from an 1810 mold. (Philadelphia Museum of Art)**

was grilled turkey, a broiler shortcut to the mammoth barbecues of colonial America, a replay of the resounding shouts of the multitudes in 1840, whose voices were now and then muffled by hot corn dodgers and the flap of banners proclaiming "Tippecanoe and Tyler Too!"

The innocence of that age is now gone. The folk aesthetic that began in country kitchens three centuries ago has undergone a vast reorientation. And yet, after all is said, the basic rules, the basic human needs, have remained the same. The old aesthetic has been rediscovered in folk art because our vision, weary from the monotony and perfection of technology, now takes delight in rustic things well made.

Folk cookery was a cookery of connectedness, of balanced parts forming a whole, at its best, a rustic thing well done. It does not shine under the Plexiglas chic of modern coffee-table culture. It has too much dirt under its nails. It survives as a wheezing museum-hybrid fare, here and there where efforts have been made to record and preserve it. Out in the subdivisions crowding against apple orchards and old cornfields gone to brush, it has found a new personality, a kind of cleaned-up look fit for magazines and mail-order catalogues. In the 1920s it was the colonial skillet and breakfast by the Victrola. Today we call it "country."

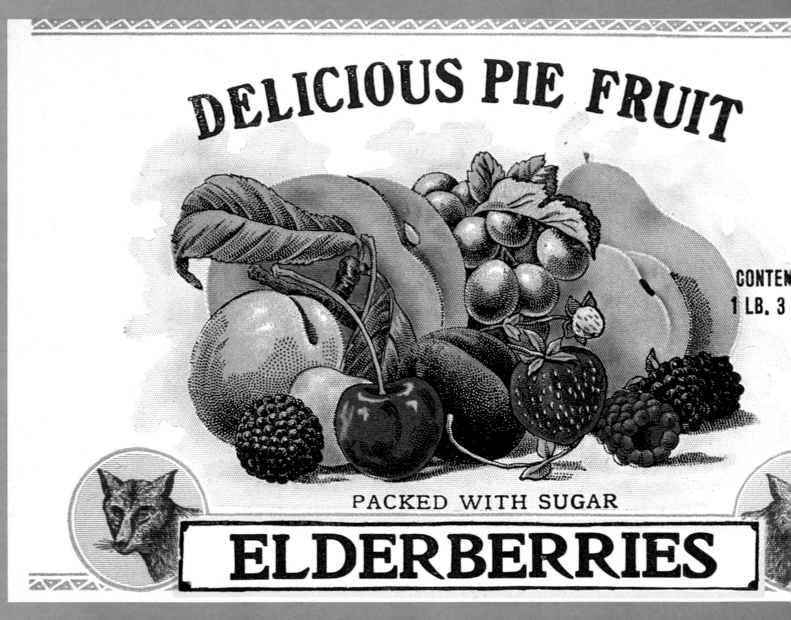

DELICIOUS PIE FRUIT

CONTEN
1 LB. 3

PACKED WITH SUGAR

ELDERBERRIES

Chromolithograph can label, circa 1915.
A recipe for elderberry pie is provided with the berries.
(Roughwood Collection)

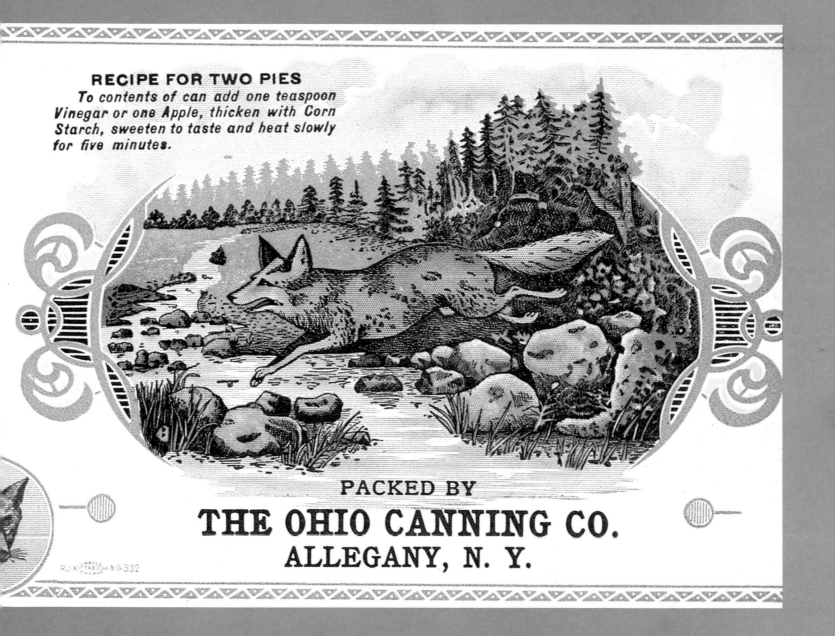

BALTIMORE CRAB GUMBO

1893

Table Talk, a household magazine edited by Sarah T. Rorer during the late nineteenth century, featured many articles and recipes inspired by the colonial revival, a favored topic with the editor. It was her way of re-creating the cookery of America's golden past for working-class Americans. This recipe, however, was submitted by one of the readers and published in response to a request for crab gumbo "such as they give you in Baltimore."

YIELD: 6 SERVINGS.

1 tablespoon unsalted butter
1 tablespoon lard or bacon drippings
8 ounces country-style smoked ham, chopped
8 ounces stewing veal, chopped
½ cup all-purpose flour
1½ cups chopped onion
2 quarts water

3 tablespoons minced parsley
1 bruised bay leaf
1 small pod cayenne pepper (see note)
12 ounces crab meat
1 cup sliced okra
1 cup brown rice
Sliced lemons for garnish

Melt the butter and lard in a deep kettle or stew pan; when it begins to sizzle, add the ham and veal. Brown the meat on all sides, then add the flour. Continue to stir and fry until all of the flour has been lightly scorched. Add the onion and stir until it wilts, then add the water, parsley, bay leaf, cayenne pepper, crab, and okra. Simmer 45 minutes, then add the brown rice. When the rice is cooked (about 30 minutes), the gumbo is ready to eat. Serve with sliced lemons.

NOTE:

If powdered cayenne is used, it will darken the gumbo. This "soiled" appearance was not considered good style by early American cooks. Powdered cayenne is also problematic because some powdered products are mild, while others are very sharp. The advantage of cooking with pods—the old way—is that they release their heat gradually, and you can remove them if the soup begins to get too peppery. You cannot reverse an overdose of pepper, and that is the easiest way to ruin a gumbo.

SOURCE: *Table Talk* 8:2 (February 1893), 64.

GRILLED TURKEY
1891

YIELD: 4 SERVINGS.

2 tablespoons sharp red vinegar
2 tablespoons mushroom catsup (see note)
2 tablespoon prepared Dijon mustard

2 tablespoons olive oil or melted unsalted butter
⅛ teaspoon cayenne pepper
4 cooked turkey legs (drumsticks or thighs)

Beat the vinegar, mushroom catsup, mustard, oil, and pepper together to form a spicy dressing. Score the turkey with a very sharp knife, then brush it with the dressing. Coat well. Set the legs under the broiler or on a gridiron over hot coals, and broil until nicely browned. Turn and baste often. Serve on a hot platter with bits of parsley butter (see below).

NOTE:
Mushroom catsup is still made in England and is available in this country at specialty food stores. Although it is not exactly the same, Worcestershire sauce may be used as a substitute.

SOURCE: H. H. Warner. *Warner's Safe Cook Book.* (Rochester, N.Y.: H. H. Warner & Co., 1891), 136.

PARSLEY BUTTER

YIELD: 4 TABLESPOONS.

4 tablespoons unsalted butter
¼ teaspoon lemon juice
2 teaspoons minced fresh parsley

⅛ teaspoon white pepper
Dash of salt

Rub the butter, lemon juice, parsley, pepper, and salt together to form a paste. Cool and chop.

TRENCH STEW

1924

YIELD: 4 TO 6 SERVINGS.

2 pounds stewing beef or mutton
2 tablespoons all-purpose flour
3 tablespoons unsalted butter
3 tablespoons brown sugar
1 cup chopped onion
2 cups water

2 tablespoons prepared Dijon mustard
1 teaspoon celery seed
6 tablespoons chopped sour gherkins or dilled cucumber pickles
Salt and pepper

Cut the meat into 1-inch cubes and dust with the flour. Melt the butter in a deep stewing kettle and brown the meat over a high heat for about 10 minutes. Add the sugar and stir until it begins to bubble and caramelize. Add the onion. When the onion is wilted, add the water and cover. Stew gently for about 30 minutes, or until the meat is tender. Then add the mustard, celery seed, and pickles. Cook for about 5 minutes and serve.

NOTE:

The mustard and the pickles are the secret to this recipe. The mustard must be delicate, not fiery, and the pickles must be sour enough to create a contrast of flavors. And even though this recipe calls for beef or mutton, it is best when made with venison.

SOURCE: Martha Washington Guild. *Martha Washington Log Cabin Cook Book/Valley Forge.* (Philadelphia: John C. Winston, 1924), 17.

Maple Candy

1894

YIELD: APPROXIMATELY 1 DOZEN PATTIES, OR
ABOUT 1 POUND OF CANDY.

1½ cups maple syrup
1 cup granulated sugar

2 tablespoons unsalted butter
1 teaspoon vanilla extract

Cook the syrup and sugar until the end of the thread stage (233° F). Remove from the heat and cool to 110° F. Do not stir. Add the butter and vanilla and beat until light and fluffy, or until mixture will hold its shape in molds or pattypans. Butter the molds and fill with the candy. Let set, then unmold. Store in airtight containers.

SOURCE: Mrs. Minnie Palmer. *The Women's Exchange Cook Book.* (Chicago: Monarch Book Company, 1894), 408.

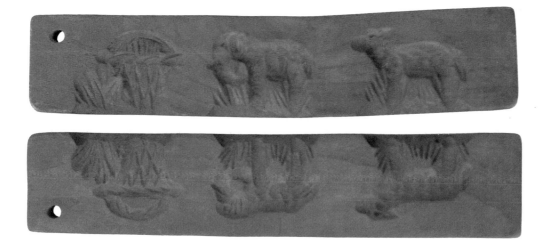

Wooden candy mold. Collection of Alice Ross.

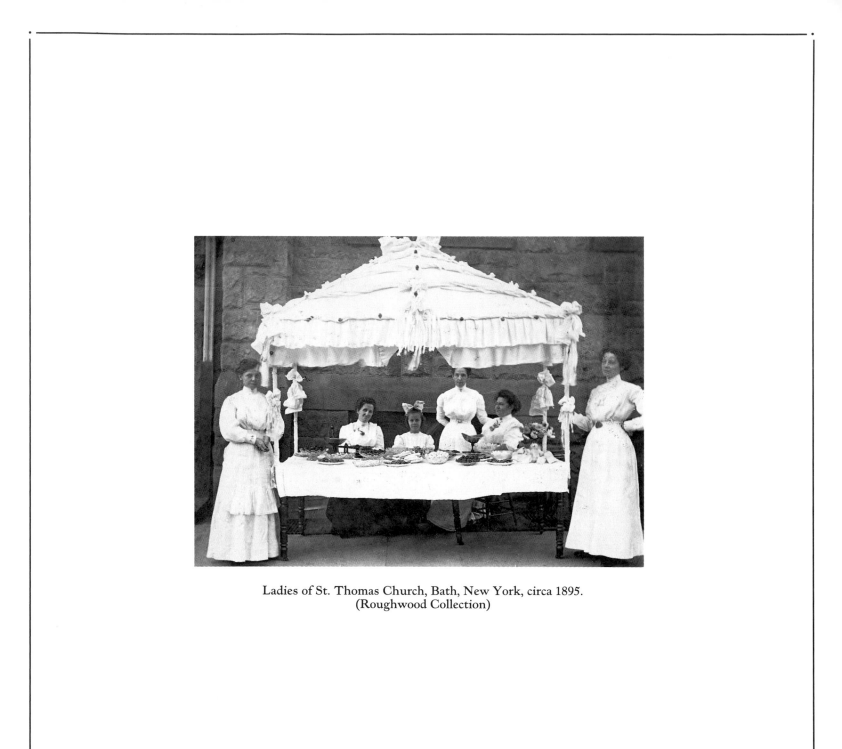

Ladies of St. Thomas Church, Bath, New York, circa 1895.
(Roughwood Collection)

Higdom is one of those recipes, like Bordeaux pickle, that appears with great regularity in Victorian charitable cookbooks. After all, it uses up garden leftovers that would otherwise go to waste with the first frost. In taste, it is a glorified form of pepper hash, and therefore it goes well with breaded fried meats and fish, and especially with fried oysters. For this reason, it was once a popular feature of church suppers and picnics. YIELD: 14 PINTS.

6 pounds green tomatoes, chopped
3 pounds onions, chopped
2 pounds white cabbage, chopped
5 green peppers, chopped
1 sweet red pepper, chopped
1 cup pickling salt
6 tablespoons mustard seed
4 tablespoons celery seed

PICKLING BRINE:

2 quarts white vinegar
3 cups sugar
2 cups spring water or bottled water
3 cinnamon sticks, broken
2 teaspoons whole cloves
2 teaspoons black peppercorns

Mix the chopped tomatoes, onions, cabbage, and peppers. Scatter the salt over this. Cover and let stand overnight to drain. The next day, press out the excess liquid, but do not rinse. Then add the mustard and celery seeds.

While the chopped vegetables are draining, combine all the ingredients for the pickling brine and bring to a hard boil. Boil 5 minutes, then cover and infuse overnight. In the morning, strain out the spices.

Put the vegetable mixture in a deep preserving pan. (If you don't have a large enough pan, divide the mixture into two equal batches.) Heat the strained pickling brine and pour over the vegetables. Cook the Higdom only until it is hot (for half a batch, approximately 15 minutes). Then fill hot, sterilized pint jars and seal. Give the jars a 15-minute water bath.

NOTE:

The pickle should mature 2 weeks before using. Store in a cool, dark place. If you have a garden with asparagus plants, throw the discarded brine on them.

SOURCE: Women of St. Thomas Church. *Parish House Receipts.* (Bath, N.Y.: Advocate Book and Job Rooms, 1892), 68.

SCOTT'S NEW YORK CHOWDER

1865

This is the famous recipe of Genio C. Scott, as originally published in the New York newspaper *Spirit of the Times*. It makes the "red" chowder now associated with Manhattan. YIELD: 6 TO 8 SERVINGS.

10 medium onions (approximately 1 pound, 12 ounces)
1½ pounds fresh cod, sea bass, or haddock
2 pounds ripe tomatoes
Approximately 1¼ pounds salt pork, cut in paper-thin slices

2 pounds potatoes, pared and quartered or sliced
2 cups coarsely crushed oyster crackers
Salt and pepper
2 cups dry red wine

Peel and parboil the onions whole in unsalted water for 10 to 15 minutes. While they are cooking, bone the fish and cut into 2-inch squares. When the onions are done, remove them from the pot and set aside. Then scald the tomatoes in the onion water, just enough to blister the skins. Remove the skins, quarter the tomatoes, and remove the seeds. Strain and reserve the cooking water.

Preheat the oven to 375° F.

Take a large, heavy baking kettle, roughly 10 inches across and 6 inches deep, and line it completely with the salt pork.

Cover the bottom with a layer of fish, then add the parboiled onions, the potatoes, tomatoes, and 1 cup of the crushed oyster crackers. Make another layer of fish and cover it with the remaining salt pork and the last cup of cracker crumbs. Add 1 to 2 cups of the reserved cooking water, or enough to bring the water to the top of the chowder. Bake for 1½ hours, or until the potatoes are tender. About 30 minutes before serving, add the wine.

SOURCE: Robert B. Roosevelt. *Superior Fishing.* (New York: Carleton, Publisher, 1865), 300–301.

OPPOSITE PAGE: Scott's New York Chowder as prepared in an iron bulge pot.

White House vinegar bottles.
Design is based on stoneware prototypes, dated 1909.

NOTES

Chapter 1

1. Elizabeth E. Lea, *Domestic Cookery* (Baltimore, 1851), 72.
2. Lea, *Domestic Cookery,* 79.
3. Lea, *Domestic Cookery,* 130.
4. William Woys Weaver, "Open-Hearth Cooking: Why All the Fuss Over Hot Ashes?" *New York Times,* April 27, 1988.
5. Caroline Gilman, *Recollections of a Southern Matron* (Philadelphia, 1859), 24.
6. Gilman, *Recollections,* 142.
7. See the advertisement of James Sweeny & Company, *Washington* [D.C.] *Gazette,* August 17, 1796. A recipe for venison ham was published in *Warner's Safe Cook Book* (Rochester, N.Y., 1891), 155–56.
8. M. E. Porter, *Mrs. Porter's New Southern Cookery Book* (Philadelphia, 1871), 339.
9. Asa Moore Janney and Werner L. Janney, *John Jay Janney's Virginia* (McClean, Va., 1978), 25.
10. *Aunt Betsy's Rule, and How It Worked* (Philadelphia, 1863), 271–72.
11. Sarah J. Hale, ed., *Modern Cookery* (Philadelphia, 1848), 214.
12. Albert Hauser, *Vom Essen und Trinken im Alten Zürich* (Zurich, 1961), 42.
13. George William Huntley, *A Story of the Sinnamahone* (Williamsport, Pa., 1936), 401.
14. *Vollständiges Nürnbergisches Koch-Buch* (Nürnberg, 1691), 578.
15. For a study of wear on clay cooking vessels, see: Ernst Helmuth Segschneider, "Pfannkuchenschüssel und Rührtopf," *Volkskunst* 4 (November 1987), 11–16.
16. See Klaus Freckmann's analysis of Nazi theories on the ethnic peculiarities of folk culture in his "Hausforschung im Dritten Reich," *Zeitschrift für Volkskunde* 78:2 (1983), 169–86; and my own analysis in English in "The Pennsylvania German House," *Winterthur Portfolio* 21:4 (1986), 243–64.
17. W. O. Atwater and C. D. Woods, *Dietary Studies with Reference to Food of the Negro in Alabama* (Washington, D.C., 1897); John Gregory Bourke, "Folk Foods of the Rio Grande Valley and Northern Mexico," *Journal of American Folklore* 8 (1895), 41–71; Hans Kurath, ed., *Linguistic Atlas of New England* (Providence, R.I., 1939–43), six volumes.
18. Eliza Leslie, *Miss Leslie's Cook Book* (Philadelphia, 1857), 455.
19. Charles Camp, "America Eats: Toward a Social Definition of American Foodways" (Philadelphia: Ph.D. dissertation, University of Pennsylvania, 1978).
20. Eliza Leslie, *Directions for Cookery* (Philadelphia, 1848), 272.
21. Harold Wentworth, *American Dialect Dictionary* (New York, 1944), 116.
22. For an Iroquois example, see: F. W. Waugh. *Iroquois Foods and Food Preparation* (Ottawa, 1916), 207, figure a. See also: Thomas G. Burton and Ambrose N. Manning, "Folk Methods of Preserving and Processing Food," *East Tennessee State University Monograph #3* (Johnson City, Tenn., 1966), 27–31.
23. Oliver Perry Medsger, *Edible Wild Plants* (New York, 1966), 196.
24. Waugh, *Iroquois Foods,* 217, figure b.
25. Jeannette Lasansky, *Central Pennsylvania Redware Pottery 1780–1904* (Lewisburg, Pa., 1979).
26. J. Roderick Moore, "Earthenware Potters Along the Great Road in Virginia and Tennessee," *The Magazine Antiques* (September 1983), 528–37.

27. Quincy J. Scarborough, "Connecticut Influence on North Carolina Stoneware," *Journal of Early Southern Decorative Arts* 10:1 (May 1984), 15–74.

28. See, for example, the advertisement of the American Basket Company, New Britain, Connecticut, in *The American Agriculturist* 28:12 (December 1868), 466.

29. Andrew S. Fuller, *The Small Fruit Culturist* (New York, 1885), 266.

30. William Woys Weaver, "White Gravies in American Popular Diet," in *Food in Change,* eds., Alexander Fenton and Eszter Kisban (Edinburgh, 1986), 41–52.

31. *Kite's Town and Country Almanac for 1822* (Philadelphia, 1821).

Chapter 2

1. Roland Barthes, "Cuisine ornemental," in *Mythologies* (Paris, 1957), 144–46.

2. Edward Walton, "Homemade Flavor," *Baker's Helper* 29:341 (August 1915), 844.

3. It does exist! For the recipe, see: *American Cookery,* 43:5 (December 1938), 310.

4. James W. Parkinson, "How to Cook Oysters," *Confectioners' Journal* 5:57 (October 1879), 23.

5. Caroline Gilman, *Recollections of a Southern Matron* (Philadelphia, 1859), 328.

6. William Byrd, *The Secret Diary of William Byrd of Westover, 1709–1712,* Louis B. Wright and Marion Tinling, eds., (Richmond, Va., 1941), vol. 1, 10.

7. "Chats in the Kitchen," *The Household* 7:6 (June 1874), 134.

8. For Bachelor's bread, see: C. H. King, "Every-Day Receipts," *The Confectioners' Journal* 3:36 (January 1878), 18.

9. For example, see Ian Quimby and Scott T. Swank, *Perspectives on American Folk Art* (New York, 1980); and Kenneth L. Ames, *Beyond Necessity: Art in the Folk Tradition* (New York, 1977).

10. William Woys Weaver, "Pie Crust Decorations in Early American Cookery," *Petit Propos Culinaires* 28 (April 1988), 57–58.

11. Amelia Simmons, *American Cookery* (Hartford, 1796), 13.

12. *Hoofland's Almanac and Family Receipt Book for 1875* (Philadelphia, 1874), unpaginated.

13. M. Lelyn Branin, *The Early Potters and Potteries of Maine* (Middletown, Conn., 1978).

14. "Cement for the Tops of Bottles or Jars," in *Agricultural Almanac for 1866* (Lancaster, Pa., 1865), unpaginated.

15. Mrs. Frances Owens, *Mrs. Owens's Cook Book and Useful Household Hints* (Chicago, 1903), 336.

16. See "Care of Sausage," *The Household* 7:7 (July 1874), 158.

17. Gervase Markham, *The English House-Wife* (London, 1675), 85.

18. See the *Eck,* Allentown *Morning Call,* January 15, 1949.

19. Refer to the firm's advertisement in *The Confectioners' Journal* 28:331 (August 1902), 99.

Chapter 3

1. "Concerning Pies," *The Household* 8:12 (December 1874), 271.
2. Eliza Leslie, *Miss Leslie's Cook Book* (Philadelphia, 1881), 474.
3. Cora, Rose, and Bob Brown, *America Cooks* (New York, 1940), 652.
4. Mary Anne Hines, Gordon Marshall, and William Woys Weaver, *The Larder Invaded* (Philadelphia, 1987), 59, 60.
5. Frances Owens, *Cook Book and Useful Household Hints* (Chicago, 1903), 56.
6. William Woys Weaver, ed., *A Quaker Woman's Cookbook* (Philadelphia, 1982).
7. Nora L. Roy, "Maple Sugaring in Southern Illinois," *Indiana Folklore* 9 (1976), 197–234.
8. Marion Lochhead, *The Scots Household in the Eighteenth Century* (Edinburgh, 1948), 221.
9. William Woys Weaver, *Sauerkraut Yankees* (Philadelphia, 1983), 191.
10. Advertisement of William Morgan, *Pennsylvania Gazette,* December 19, 1732.
11. John Bennett, "Food and Culture in Southern Illinois," *American Sociological Review* 7 (1942), 645–60.
12. Pliny Durant, *The History of Clinton County, Ohio* (Chicago, 1882), 698.
13. Allan Bogue, *From Prairie to Cornbelt* (Chicago, 1968).
14. Durant, *History,* 698.
15. "How We Bake Our Bread," *American Agriculturist* (June 1873), 225.
16. "American Diet," *The Household* 7:2 (February 1874), 32.
17. Catherine Beecher, *Miss Beecher's Domestic Receipt Book* (New York, 1846), 102–3.
18. *The Household* 7:8 (August 1874), 183.

Chapter 4

1. *Pennsylvania Gazette,* April 9, 1747.
2. *Democrat and Herald* (Wilmington, Ohio), May 15, 1840.
3. See Calvin Trillin, *American Fried* (New York, 1975); and A. C. Martin, "Patriotism and Fried Chicken," *Sewanee Review* 37 (January 1929), 34–37.
4. Lucy Larcom, *A New England Girlhood* (Boston, 1889), 98–99.
5. Byrd, *Secret Diary,* vol. 1, 549.
6. Frances S. Osgood, *The Poetry of Flowers* (New York, 1846), 263.
7. Peter Brears, *The Gentlewoman's Kitchen* (Wakefield, 1984), 12.
8. John Widdowson, "The Things They Say About Food," *Folk Life: A Journal of Ethnological Studies* (Leeds) 13 (1975), 10.
9. Caroline Gilman, *Lady's Annual Register* (Boston, 1838), 96.
10. Theodore W. Bean, *History of Montgomery County, Pennsylvania* (Philadelphia, 1884), Appendix, xxiv.
11. McCool died in Doylestown Township, Bucks County, Pennsylvania, on July 4, 1890. Unidentified newspaper clipping from a Bucks County scrapbook. Private collection.
12. Tyrone Power, *Impressions of America* (Philadelphia, 1836), vol. 1, 105.
13. Simmons, *American Cookery,* 35.
14. See the advertisement of James Y. Watkins & Son, *The Confectioners' Journal* 35:288 (January 1899), 110.
15. Edith Hörandner, *Model* (Munich, 1982), 50.

Chapter 5

1. Henry Glassie, *Pattern in the Material Folk Culture of the Eastern United States* (Philadelphia, 1968), 71–73.
2. *Warner's Safe Cook Book* (Rochester, N.Y., 1891), 171.
3. *Warner's,* 170.
4. She was particularly adamant about the decline of bread. See her chapter on "Good Cooking" in Catherine E. Beecher and Harriet Beecher Stowe, *The American Woman's Home* (New York, 1869).
5. "The Customary Method for Making Potash used in the State of New-York," *Pennsylvania Gazette,* August 6, 1788.
6. Ellen Paul Denker, "Ceramics at the Crossroads," *Staten Island Historian* 3: 3/4 (Winter/Spring, 1986), 21–35.
7. See, for example, the pamphlet cookbook *Hecker's Croton Flour Mills* (New York, 1869), unpaginated.
8. Maria Parloa, *Miss Parloa's Kitchen Companion* (Boston, 1887), 4.
9. According to the Boston city directory for 1859, Waterman was both a tinware manufacturer with a factory at 120 Lincoln Street and co-owner, with Charles B. Lothrop, of Nathaniel Waterman & Co., a house-furnishing store at 8 Bedford Street. Waterman held patents on a wide range of kitchen utensils and appliances, including an early refrigerator.
10. Durant, *History,* 383.
11. Sarah T. Rorer, *Mrs. Rorer's New Cook Book* (Philadelphia, 1902), 513.
12. See the advertisement in *The American Agriculturist* 28:12 (December 1868), 472.
13. See: "Inventor of Angel Cake Dead," *The National Baker* 4:38 (March 15, 1899), 16.
14. See their brochure: *Cream Puff Bakery Yeast: For Making Light, Wholesome and Nutritious Bread* (Philadelphia, 1876), which was given away at the U.S. Centennial.
15. *Connecticut Journal,* May 25, 1796.
16. *Columbian Centinel* (Boston), March 16, 1796.
17. Branin, *The Early Potters,* 155.
18. See: Andrew L. and Kate B. Winton, *Norwalk Potteries* (Canaan, Conn., 1981).
19. *The Household* 7:3 (March 1874), 60.
20. Parloa, *Miss Parloa's,* 35.
21. Ladies' Society of St. Mark's Lutheran Church, *Mohawk Valley Cook Book* (Utica, N.Y., 1889), 65.

Chapter 6

1. Recipe of Mrs. Joseph E. Culver, New Haven, Connecticut, in: *Larkin Housewives' Cook Book* (Buffalo, N.Y., 1915), 67.
2. "Cooking in Stoneware: The Renaissance of Kitchen Pottery," *Table Talk* 14:8 (August 1899), 306–8.
3. The word *chowder* comes from the French *chaudiere,* meaning "boiler" or "kettle." In terms of early American culture, chowders were any form of stew prepared in cauldrons out of doors, usually on fishing boats or along beaches. It was something prepared by men under rustic circumstances, as in the eighteenth-century Massachusetts recipe preserved by Charlotte Mason: "A Sea Dish, called Chouder." See Charlotte Mason, *The Ladies' Assistant* (London, 1787), 179.

SELECTED BIBLIOGRAPHY

Agricultural Almanac for 1855. Lancaster, Pa.: Printed by John Baer & Son, 1854.

Agricultural Almanac for 1866. Lancaster, Pa.: Printed by John Baer & Son, 1865.

Agricultural Almanac for 1869. Lancaster, Pa.: Printed by John Baer & Son, 1868.

The American Family Keepsake. Boston: H. B. Skinner & J. B. Hall, 1848.

The American Housewife. New York: Collins, Keese & Co., 1839.

Ames, Kenneth. *Beyond Necessity. Art in the Folk Tradition.* New York: W. W. Norton, 1977.

The Approved Recipe Book. Plainfield, N.J.: M. F. Cushing, 1839.

Atwater, W. O., and C. D. Woods. *Dietary Studies with Reference to Food of the Negro in Alabama in 1895 and 1896.* Washington, D.C.: U.S. Department of Agriculture, Office of Experimental Stations, Bulletin 38, 1897.

Aunt Betsy's Rule and How It Worked. Philadelphia: Presbyterian Board of Publication, 1863.

Barthes, Roland. *Mythologies.* Paris: Editions du Seuil, 1957.

Bartis, Peter, David S. Cohen, and Gregory Dowd. *Folklife Resources in New Jersey.* Washington, D.C.: American Folklife Center, 1985.

Bean, Theodore W. *History of Montgomery County, Pennsylvania.* Philadelphia: Everts & Peck, 1884.

Beecher, Catherine. *Miss Beecher's Domestic Receipt Book.* New York: Harper & Brothers, 1846.

————and Harriet Beecher Stowe. *The American Woman's Home.* New York: J. B. Ford & Co., 1869.

Benes, Peter. *Foodways in the Northeast.* Boston: Boston University Scholarly Publications, 1984.

Bennett, John, H. L. Smith, and H. Passin. "Food and Culture in Southern Illinois." *American Sociological Review* 7 (1942).

Bickham & Huffman. *Cream Puff Baking Yeast: For Making Light, Wholesome and Nutritious Bread, Biscuit, Cakes, Pastry, Dumplings, etc.* Philadelphia: Holland & Edgar, 1876.

Bogue, Allan. *From Prairie to Cornbelt.* Chicago: Quadrangle Books, 1968.

Boston Directory for the Year Ending June 30, 1860. Boston: Adams, Sampson, and Co., 1859.

Bourke, John Gregory. "The Folk Foods of the Rio Grande Valley and Northern Mexico." *Journal of American Folklore* 8 (1895).

Branin, M. Lelyn. *The Early Potters and Potteries of Maine.* Middletown, Conn.: Wesleyan University Press, 1978.

Brears, Peter. *The Gentlewoman's Kitchen: Great Food in Yorkshire 1650–1750.* Wakefield (England): Wakefield Historical Publications, 1984.

Brown, Cora, Rose, and Bob. *America Cooks.* New York: W. W. Norton, 1940.

Burton, Thomas G., and Ambrose N. Manning. "Folk Methods of Preserving and Processing Food." *East Tennessee State University Monograph 3.* Johnson City, Tenn.: Institute of Regional Studies, 1966.

Byrd, William. *The Secret Diary of William Byrd of Westover, 1709–1712.* 2 vols. Louis B. Wright and Marion Tinling, eds. Richmond, Va.: Dietz Press, 1941 and 1942.

Camp, Charles. "America Eats: Toward a Social Definition of American Foodways." Philadelphia: Ph.D. dissertation, University of Pennsylvania, 1978.

Cookery As It Should Be; A New Manual of Dining Room and Kitchen. Philadelphia: Willis P. Hazard, 1855.

Cooper, Dr. Thomas, ed. *The Domestic Encyclopedia*. 3 vols. Philadelphia: Abraham Small, 1821.

Cummings, Richard Osborn. *The American and His Food: A History of Food Habits in the United States*. Chicago: University of Chicago Press, 1940.

Davis, Gerald L. "Afro-American Coil Basketry in Charleston County, South Carolina." In *American Folklife,* edited by Don Yoder. Austin: University of Texas Press, 1976.

Denker, Ellen Paul. "Ceramics at the Crossroads: American Pottery at New York's Gateway, 1750–1900." *Staten Island Historian,* 3: 3/4 (Winter/Spring 1986).

Durant, Pliny A., ed. *The History of Clinton County, Ohio*. Chicago: W. H. Beers & Co., 1882.

Earle, Alice Morse. *Colonial Days in Old New York*. New York: Charles Scribner's Sons, 1896.

East Marlboro Branch of County Auxiliary. *Our Favorite Recipes*. Kennett Square, Pa.: privately printed, 1915.

Ellison, Julia, ed. *Cook Book Compiled by the Members of "The Sojourner's Club."* Kirksville, Mo.: Journal Printing, 1915.

Ellsworth, Mahlon W., and F. B. Dickerson. *The Successful Housekeeper*. Harrisburg, Pa.: Pennsylvania Publishing Co., 1883.

Esopus Methodist Episcopal Church. *The Cook's Manual and Buyer's Director*. Rondout, N.Y.: Kingston Freeman, 1891.

The Family's Guide. Cortland, N.Y.: C. W. Mason, 1833.

Fenton, Alexander, and Eszter Kisban, eds. *Food in Change*. Edinburgh: John Donald, 1986.

Freckmann, Klaus. "Hausforschung im Dritten Reich." *Zeitschrift für Volkskunde* 78:2 (1983).

Fuller, Andrew S. *The Small Fruit Culturist*. New York: Orange Judd, 1885.

Gibson, Marietta P. *Mrs. Charles H. Gibson's Maryland and Virginia Cook Book*. Baltimore: John Murphy & Co., 1894.

Gilman, Caroline. *The Lady's Annual Register and Housewife's Memorandum-Book*. Boston: T. H. Carter, 1838.

————*Recollections of a Southern Matron*. Philadelphia: G. G. Evans, 1859.

Girardey, George. *Höchst Nützliches Handbuch über Kochkunst*. Cincinnati, Ohio: J. A. James, 1842.

Glassie, Henry. *Pattern in the Material Folk Culture of the Eastern United States*. Philadelphia: University of Pennsylvania Press, 1968.

Hale, Sarah J., ed. *Modern Cookery in All Its Branches, by Eliza Acton*. Philadelphia: Lea and Blanchard, 1848.

Hauser, Albert. *Vom Essen und Trinken im Alten Zürich*. Zürich: Verlag Berichthaus, 1961.

Hearn, Lafcadio. *La Cuisine Creole*. New Orleans, La.: F. F. Hansell & Bro., 1885.

Hecker's Croton Flour Mills. New York: Hecker & Brother, 1869.

Hines, Mary Anne, Gordon Marshall, and William Woys Weaver. *The Larder Invaded: Reflections on Three Centuries of Philadelphia Food and Drink*. Philadelphia: Library Company of Philadelphia, 1987.

Hoofland's Almanac and Family Receipt Book for 1875. Philadelphia: Johnson, Halloway & Co., 1874.

Hooker, Margaret H. *Ye Gentlewoman's Housewifery*. New York: Dodd, Mead and Company, 1896.

Hörandner, Edith. *Model. Geschnitzte Formen für Lebkuchen, Spekulatius und Springerle*. Munich: D. W. Callwey, 1982.

Huntley, George William. *A Story of the Sinnamahone*. Williamsport, Pa.: Williamsport Printing, 1936.

Janney, Werner L., and Asa Moore Janney, eds. *John Jay Janney's Virginia.* McClean, Va.: EPM Publications, Inc., 1978.

King, C. H. "Every-Day Receipts." *Confectioners' Journal,* 3:36 (January 1878), 18.

Kite's Town and Country Almanac for 1822. Philadelphia: Benjamin & Thomas Kite, 1821.

Kurath, Hans. *A Word Geography of the Eastern United States.* Ann Arbor: The University of Michigan Press, 1970.

———*Linguistic Atlas of New England.* 6 vols. Providence, R. I.: Brown University, 1939–43.

Ladies of the First Presbyterian Church. *Presbyterian Cook Book.* Wheeling, W.V.: F. H. Crago, 1889.

Ladies' Society of St. Mark's Lutheran Church, Canajoharie, N.Y. *Mohawk Valley Cook Book.* Utica, N.Y.: Press of J. C. Childs, 1889.

Lancaster, (Pa.) General Hospital "Benefit" Cook Book. Lancaster, Pa.: Conn & Slote, 1912.

Larcom, Lucy. *A New England Girlhood.* Boston: Houghton Mifflin, 1889.

Larkin Company. *Larkin Housewives' Cook Book.* Buffalo, N.Y.: Larkin Co., 1915.

Lasansky, Jeannette. *Central Pennsylvania Redware Pottery 1780–1904.* Lewisburg, Pa.: Union County Oral Traditions Project, 1979.

Lea, Elizabeth E. *Domestic Cookery, Useful Receipts and Hints to Young Housekeepers.* Baltimore: Cushings and Bailey, 1851.

Leslie, Eliza. *New Directions for Cookery.* Philadelphia: Carey & Hart, 1848.

———. *New Receipts for Cooking.* Philadelphia: T. B. Peterson, 1852.

———. *Miss Leslie's Cook Book.* Philadelphia: T. B. Peterson, 1881.

Lochhead, Marion. *The Scot's Household in the Eighteenth Century.* Edinburgh: The Moray Press, 1948.

Markham, Gervase. *The English House-Wife.* London: Printed by F. Streater, 1675.

Marshall, Josiah T. *The Farmer's and Emigrant's Hand-Book.* New York: D. Appleton & Co., 1845.

Martha Washington Guild. *Martha Washington Log Cabin Cook Book/Valley Forge.* Philadelphia: John C. Winston, 1924.

Martin, A. C. "Patriotism and Fried Chicken." *Sewanee Review* 37 (January 1929), 34–37.

Mason, Charlotte. *The Ladies' Assistant for Regulating and Supplying the Table.* London: J. Walter, 1787.

McCulloch-Williams, Martha. *Dishes & Beverages of the Old South.* Knoxville, Tenn.: University of Tennessee Press, 1988.

Medsger, Oliver Perry. *Edible Wild Plants.* New York: Macmillan, 1966.

Miller, Dr. C. C. *The Food Value of Honey. Honey Cooking-Recipes.* Medina, Ohio: A. I. Root Co., ca. 1910.

Montgomery, Morton L. *Historical and Biographical Annals of Berks County.* Chicago: J. H. Beers, 1909.

Moore, J. Roderick. "Earthenware Potters Along the Great Road in Virginia and Tennessee." *The Magazine Antiques* (September 1983).

Mumford, Lewis. "Back to the Table." *The New Republic,* August 15, 1928.

National Rice Milling Co. *Gold Medal Rice Cook Book.* New Orleans: National Rice Milling Co., 1907.

The New Family Receipt Book. New Haven, Conn.: Howe & Spalding, 1819.

Osgood, Frances S. *The Poetry of Flowers.* New York: J. C. Riker, 1846.

Owens, Frances E. *Mrs. Owens's Cook Book and Useful Household Hints.* Chicago: American Publishing House, 1903.

Palmer, Mrs. Minnie. *The Women's Exchange Cook Book*. Chicago: Monarch Book Co., 1894.

Parker, Deborah H., and Jane E. Weeden. *Indiana W.C.T.U. Hadley Industrial School Cook Book*. Indianapolis: Organizer Print, 1884.

Parkinson, James W. "How to Cook Oysters." *The Confectioners' Journal* 5:57 (October 1879), 22–23.

Parloa, Maria. *Miss Parloa's Kitchen Companion*. Boston: Estes and Lauriat, 1887.

Peasant's Repast: Or, The Benevolent Physician. Philadelphia: Jacob Johnson, 1808.

Porter, Mrs. M. E. *Mrs. Porter's New Southern Cookery Book*. Philadelphia: John E. Potter, 1871.

Power, Tyrone. *Impressions of America During the Years 1833, 1834, and 1835*. 2 vols. Philadelphia: Carey and Lea, 1836.

Queen of the Kitchen. Baltimore: Lucas Brothers, 1870.

Quimby, Ian, and Scott T. Swank. *Perspectives on American Folk Art*. New York: W. W. Norton & Co., 1980.

Roosevelt, Robert B. *Superior Fishing*. New York: Carleton, Publisher, 1865.

Rorer, Sarah T. *Colonial Recipes*. Philadelphia: Arnold & Co., 1894.

———. *Mrs. Rorer's New Cook Book*. Philadelphia: Arnold & Co., 1902.

Roy, Nora Leonard. "Maple Sugaring in Southern Indiana: A Descriptive Study of the Technology of Four Maple Sugar Makers." *Indiana Folklore* 9 (1976), 197–234.

Scarborough, Quincy J. "Connecticut Influence on North Carolina Stoneware: The Webster School of Potters." *Journal of Early Southern Decorative Arts* 10:1 (May 1984), 15–74.

———. *North Carolina Decorated Stoneware: The Webster School of Folk Potters*. Fayetteville, N.C.: The Scarborough Press, 1966.

Segschneider, Ernst Helmuth. "Pfannkuchenschüssel und Rührtopf." *Volkskunst* 4 (November 1987), 11–16.

Simmons, Amelia. *American Cookery*. Hartford: Hudson and Goodwin, 1796.

Singleton, Esther. *Social New York Under the Georges 1714–1776*. New York: D. Appleton and Co., 1902.

Standard American Cook Book. Springfield, Oh.: Crowell & Kirkpatrick, 1897.

Swett, Lucia Gray. *New England Breakfast Breads, Luncheon and Tea Biscuits*. Boston: Lee and Shepard, 1891.

Tennet, Mrs. E. R. *House-Keeping in the Sunny South*. Atlanta, Ga.: James P. Harrison & Co., 1885.

Trillin, Calvin. *American Fried*. New York: Penguin Books, 1975.

Trimble, William, ed. *Made in Western Pennsylvania. Early Decorative Arts: An Exhibition*. Pittsburgh: Historical Society of Western Pennsylvania, 1982.

Truman & Shaw. *Catalogue of Housekeepers', Builders and Miscellaneous Hardware and Tools*. Philadelphia: Kildare, Printer, 1865.

Tutt, William H. *Dr. Tutt's Manual of Valuable Information and Useful Receipts*. New York: Published by Dr. William H. Tutt, 1873.

Vaughn, Kate B. *Culinary Echoes from Dixie*. Cincinnati, Ohio: The McDonald Press, 1914.

Vollständiges Nürnbergisches Koch-Buch. Nürnberg: In Verlegung Wolfgang Moritz Endters, 1691.

Walton, Edward. "Homemade Flavor." *Baker's Helper* 29:341 (August 1915), 844.

Warner, H. H. *Warner's Safe Cook Book*. Rochester, N.Y.: H. H. Warner & Co., 1891.

Waugh, F. W. *Iroquois Foods and Food Preparation*. Ottawa: Government Printing Bureau, 1916.

Weaver, William Woys. *A Quaker Woman's Cookbook*. Philadelphia: University of Pennsylvania Press, 1982.

———. *Sauerkraut Yankees*. Philadelphia: University of Pennsylvania Press, 1983.

———. "White Gravies in American Popular Diet." In *Food in Change,* edited by Alexander Fenton and Eszter Kisban. Edinburgh: John Donald, 1986, 41–52.

———. "The Pennsylvania German House." *Winterthur Portfolio* 21:4 (1986), 243–64.

———. "Pie Crust Decorations in Early American Cookery." *Petits Propos Culinaires* 28 (April 1988), 57–58.

———. "Open-Hearth Cookery: Why All the Fuss Over Hot Ashes?" *New York Times,* April 27, 1988.

Wentworth, Harold. *American Dialect Dictionary*. New York: Thomas Y. Crowell, 1944.

Widdowson, John P. A. "The Things They Say About Food." *Folk Life: A Journal of Ethnological Studies* (Leeds) 13 (1975), 5–12.

Winton, Andrew L. and Kate B. *Norwalk Potteries*. Canaan, N.H.: Phoenix Publishing, 1981.

Women of St. Thomas Church. *Parish House Receipts*. Bath, N.Y.: Advocate Book and Job Rooms, 1892.

Zug, Charles G. *The Traditional Pottery of North Carolina*. Chapel Hill: The Ackland Art Museum/University of North Carolina Press, 1981.

Manuscripts

Langston, Mrs. T. L. "Cook Book." Atlanta, Georgia, October 28, 1870. Roughwood Collection.

Nutt, Samuel. "Savorall Rare Sacrets and Choyce Curiossityes." Chester County, Pennsylvania 1702–37. Unpublished Memorandum Book. Chester County Historical Society, West Chester, Pennsylvania.

Sargent, Mrs. E. F. "Cookbook." Walpole, New Hampshire, ca. 1865. Roughwood Collection.

Underhill, Phebe W. "Receipt Book." Long Island, New York, ca. 1834–50. Roughwood Collection.

COLLECTOR'S·GUIDE·TO·
OBJECTS·ILLUSTRATED·IN·THIS·BOOK

PAGE 28
Cook Pot or "Hominy Pot"
Ellis Griffith
Circa 1790–1810
American
Cast Iron
D: (rim) 9", H: 8¾"
Private Collection

PAGE 31 (left to right)
Baking Dish
Anonymous
Circa 1780–1820
Vermont
Redware
L: 11½", W: 9", H: 1½"
Private Collection

Wooden Spoon
Anonymous
Circa 1800
American
Chestnut
L: 9"
Private Collection

Salt Cellar
Anonymous
Circa 1795
New Geneva, Pennsylvania
Violet Glass
D: (base) 1¾", H: 2⅞"
Private Collection

PAGE 32
Baking Pot with Lid
Anonymous
Circa 1815–1825
Pennsylvania
Redware
H: 203 cm, D: 354 cm
Collection of the Philadelphia
Museum of Art

PAGE 35 (left to right)
Aspic or Souse Mold
Anonymous
Circa 1885
American
Copper
H: 10½", D: (rim) 8¼"
Private Collection

Aspic or Souse Mold
Anonymous
Circa 1880
American
Tin
H: 5¾", D: (rim) 7¼"
Private Collection

PAGE 39
Butter Paddle or "Spade"
Signed T.F.S.
Circa 1840
New York or Western Vermont
Bird's Eye Maple
L: 12", W: 4"
Private Collection

PAGE 43
Cookie Cutter
Anonymous
Circa 1840–1860
Pennsylvania
Tin
H: 5⅝", W: 7¼"
Collection of the Philadelphia
Museum of Art

PAGE 45
Stone Firkin or Cake Crock
Anonymous
Circa 1870
American
Stoneware
H: 6⅝", D: 10⅝"
Collection of the Henry Francis
du Pont Winterthur Museum

PAGE 47 (left to right)
Preserve Pot with Parchment
Cover
Anonymous
Circa 1800
Hudson Valley
Redware, Albany slip
H: 5¼", D: (rim) 5"
Private Collection

Gherkin or Chow-Chow Jar
Anonymous
Circa 1870
Ohio
Stoneware
H: 9⅜", D: (base) 4⅝"
Private collection

PAGE 48 (left to right)
Preserve Pot
Anonymous
Circa 1830
Ohio
Stoneware
H: 5¼"
Private Collection

Peoria Tomato Jar
Anonymous
Circa 1865–1875
Illinois or Indiana
Brown glazed stoneware
H: 8¾", D: (base) 4"
Private Collection

Fruit Jar (1 quart)
John Bell
Circa 1855–1860
Waynesboro, Pennsylvania
Yellowware
H: 7½", D: (base) 5¼"
Private Collection

Pickle Jar
H. H. Melick
Circa 1876
Roseville, Ohio
Stoneware
H: 11¼", D: (base) 6¼"
Private Collection

Bottle
Henry Glazer
Circa 1835
Huntingdon, Pennsylvania
Stoneware
H: 8⅜", D: (base) 3½"
Private Collection

PAGE 49
The "Gem" Preserve Jar
Hero Glass Works
Circa 1870
Philadelphia
Glass, original tin lid
H: 7"
Private Collection

PAGE 53 (left to right)
Storage Jar
Anonymous
Circa 1820
Bucks County, Pennsylvania
Redware, glazed interior
H: 12¼", D: (base) 7"
Private Collection

Jar
Anonymous
Circa 1790–1825
Baltimore
Stoneware
H: 13¼", D: (base) 8¾"
Private Collection

Stoneware Firkin (½ gallon)
Cowden and Wilcox
Circa 1885
Harrisburg, Pennsylvania
Stoneware
H: 4⅞", D: (rim) 9¼"
Private Collection

Storage Crock
J. Swank & Company
Circa 1880
Johnstown, Pennsylvania
Stoneware
H: 9⅜", D: (rim) 10¼"
Private Collection

PAGE 55 (left to right)
Beer Bottle
Anonymous
Circa 1800–1815
Ohio
Black glass
H: 7½"
Private Collection

Platter
Anonymous
Circa 1795–1815
English
Creamware
L: 11½", W: 9¼"
Private Collection

Sauce Tureen
Anonymous
Circa 1795–1815
English
Creamware
H: 3"
Private Collection

RECIPE INDEX

SUBJECT INDEX

Page references in italics refer to illustrations.